WALKING IN
PEAKLAND

ABOUT THE AUTHOR

Roger Redfern is a well-known mountaineer and photo-journalist whose articles appear regularly in publications including *High*, *The Great Outdoors*, *Peak District Magazine*, *Peakland Walker*, *The Guardian* and *The People's Friend*. A founder tutor of the former Mountaineering Association, he has climbed all over Britain and the Alps, and in Africa and north-eastern USA. A former editor of the mountaineering magazine *Mountain Craft* (later *Mountain*), he has written 29 other books, including the Cicerone guide *Walking in the Hebrides*.

WALKING IN PEAKLAND

by

Roger Redfern

CICERONE PRESS
MILNTHORPE, CUMBRIA, LA7 7PY
www.cicerone.co.uk

Text and illustrations © 2001 R. Redfern
ISBN 1 85284 315 2
A catalogue record for this book is available from the British Library.

ACKNOWLEDGEMENT

I am indebted to Gill Skeemer for help with the typescript.

Advice to Readers

Readers are advised that whilst every effort is taken by the author to ensure the accuracy of this guidebook, changes can occur which may affect the contents. It is advisable to check locally on transport, accommodation, shops, etc., though even rights of way can be altered. The publisher would welcome notes of any such changes.

Front cover: *On the Rocking Stone, Howden Moors (Walk 6)*

CONTENTS

KEY TO MAPS

 ROUTE

 UPLAND AREAS

 SUMMIT

 LAKE

 MAIN ROAD

 BRIDGE

 MINOR ROAD OR FARM TRACK

 CHURCH

 ROUTE DIRECTION

 WOOD

 RIVER

 PARKING PLACE

 RAILWAY

 BUILDING

INTRODUCTION

When *Rambles in Peakland* – my first hardback title – first appeared there were few walking guides to the area then in print. Since that time there has been a plethora of publications on the subject, of widely varying content. Many of them simply provide route-finding data with no additional research.

The Peak District, first British National Park and now reputedly the second most visited on earth, got its name from the 'Pecsaetan', the colonist tribe who lived here and were first recorded in a seventh-century survey. Certainly it is not a district of 'peaks' in the modern sense of the word – few highland areas of Britain have less claim to peaky topography than this one.

The three predominant rocks of Peakland are carboniferous limestone, millstone grit and coal measures. The ancient limestone provides the 'white peak' with its white-walled upland and villages, and deep, sometimes dry valleys. The millstone grit provides wilder, loftier country, with steep 'edges' and plateaux and warm-coloured farmsteads. The coal measures, especially along the eastern borders of the National Park, have been moulded into typically rolling, verdant, hedge-and-wood, hill-and-vale countryside.

Along with the 'king of the ramblers', G.H.B. Ward, I much prefer the millstone grit and coal measures scenically and for walking on. Routes tend to be restricted to the relatively fertile fields of the limestone upland rather than over the open uplands on the grit, and the 'white dales' (as of Dove and Wye) provide natural 'route-ways' for dense weekend and holiday populations compared with the wonderfully wide and lonely hills of the surrounding rock formations. Ward once put it well:

'From the point of view of walkers like myself a great deal of the charm of a ramble is lost when you are cooped in a cleft where there is too little air, and sun has double power. In fact, the freshness and invigoration of the moorland are lost, and walking is a task rather than a spontaneous delight. It is just as well to

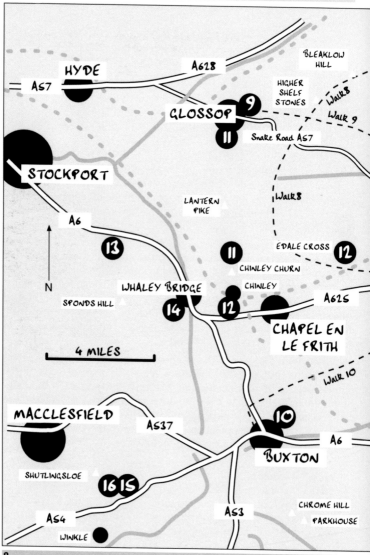

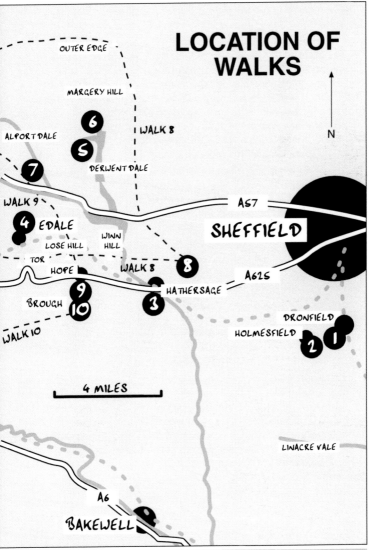

LOCATION OF WALKS

OUTER EDGE

MARGERY HILL

ALPORT DALE

6

5

WALK 8

DERWENT DALE

N

7

WALK 9

A57

SHEFFIELD

4 EDALE

WINN HILL

LOSE HILL

TOR

HOPE

WALK 8

8

A625

HATHERSAGE

9

BROUGH

10

3

DRONFIELD

HOLMESFIELD

2 **1**

WALK 10

4 MILES

LINACRE VALE

A6

BAKEWELL

remember this before setting forth on a summer-time ramble through the dales, and to allow yourself more time than if you were keeping on the breezy 'tops'.

The point of this book is to provide walkers with interesting routes and at the same time to give details of local history and other human interest and to mention some of the features to be seen in distant views. These details are by no means exhaustive, but I hope they will provide an incentive to walkers to find out more about the countryside over which they are walking. I have not restricted routes to within the boundary of the National Park – the first walk never enters it and some enter and leave it to suit the route chosen.

The book describes 16 routes: it starts with walks in the east of the region and generally works westwards, with a few deviations to north and south. All the walks are circular, except for three linear routes – 9, 10 and 12. The book also has four sections giving general background information on four areas of the Peak District.

Walk lengths vary greatly to suit the individual and the mood, and range between half a dozen and over forty miles. An outline of the route and other details, including a suggested parking place, are given at the beginning of each route description.

Some of the lower level, shorter routes require only limited walking experience, while the longer ones at higher altitudes require previous experience of walking in high places and, of course, a degree of phys-ical fitness. On the high plateaux areas, especially, a compass and the skill to use it properly are also essential.

Each route is accompanied by a sketch map, but these are for general guidance only; an OS map is an essential companion. The two most useful maps are the OS 1:25,000 Outdoor Leisure Sheets 1 (The Peak District – Dark Peak Area) and 24 (The Peak District – White Peak Area), though one or two routes (such as Walks 1 and 2) require the OS 1:25,000 Pathfinder Sheets specified at the beginning of the relevant walk. Placenames marked on the sketch maps are highlighted in bold type in the text to aid route orientation.

The Magic of Barlow Vale

Stand upon the green brow of Monk Wood on any clear day of the year and look southwards to the vale beneath. Look eastwards to the open mouth of the vale, at its conurbated joining with the Drone valley. Look westwards to a rural world, of trees and tilted fields and old stone and the distant brown line of the Pennine gritstone moors.

Barlow Vale is almost 6 miles (9.5 km) long, from the edge of Big Moor down the open way to Sheepbridge, dirty and noisy with industry, road and rail. But immediately upon entering the valley-sides the bustle is left behind; the Barlow Brook clears and brick banks become butter-burr banks, ochre turns to crystal. At its source on the heather moor the brook is 930 feet (283 metres) above sea level; at its confluence with the Drone by Sheepbridge, clattering and grey, it is only 240 feet (73 metres) above the sea. The brook is generally known as Barlow Brook throughout its length though, correctly, it is Smeekley Brook in its upper reaches, Millthorpe Brook by Cordwell and Millthorpe, Dunston Brook from Millthorpe to Crowhole, and Barlow Brook only from Crowhole to its confluence with Sud Brook, from where it becomes Brierley Brook, named after the woods to the north.

The valley as a whole does not give the appearance of immaturity, being relatively wide and of smooth contour. It is 2½ miles (4 km) across at its widest, between Holmesfield and Grange Hill. Physiographically oyster-like, the narrowing at the mouth opens to the wider sweeps between Barlow village and mid-Monk Wood, then narrows vice-like by Common Side and Crowhole. Westwards the valley opens, receiving many children – Hollin Wood Brook, Pingle Dike and Burrs Brook from the south and numerous rivulets from the more regular contours of the northern slopes.

The whole trough is essentially pastoral, in the Beethovian sense; classical green of deep hedgerows and tall trees, hawthorn and ash. Rolling hills unfold to the valley floor, clouds pile cumulus-wise above the open brows. This is the home of vigorous youth; this is the home of sentimental older age; the home of schoolboy and sage, enjoyed by all beneath a bespeckled cirro-cumulus sky. There is magic round every hedge-bend, beyond every deep turn in every brook falling from the tops. Here lives Titania, tripping by meadow-walk and woodland stile.

Monk Wood was once the biggest area of natural woodland in these parts: green spires leaning to the sky from deep bracken-ways. It is sub-divided into many lesser woods, at least in name: Loundes Wood, Little Loundes Wood and Brierley Wood above the Drone; Roughpiece, Blackpiece and Roecar Woods on the northern valley slopes; Grasscroft and Lees Woods annexed to the north and west. Most of their hundreds of acres have gone – on timber lorries or up in smoke – but the ruins remain; and nature is the only true healer.

To the newcomer the charm of this woodland may not be conspic-uous; now few deciduous giants soar above a floral wonderland floor. But for one who has known these slopes since childhood much of the magic still remains. Gone is the Kingsleyan mystery of the Green Pond in Blackpiece, gone the glimmering green of the Beech Avenue, incred-ibly high to my boy's eyes, the mine heap of the Blue Mountain which was buried (except on top) by colonising birch and which revealed a Promised Land view away to Brampton Woods and Holymoorside on summer days of unbelievable heat and dreamy cloud-islands. In memory these things remain as impossibly beautiful – doubtless far more perfect than they actually were. It is the God-given 'grace of forgetting' that makes 'the snows of December gleam gold with the sun of July'.

Since the mid-seventies, of course, the central part of the wood has been ruined by the construction of the Unstone–Dronfield by-pass (A61). It scythes right through this former wonderland bringing noise, move-ment, pollution. Corners, though, retain the magic.

Monk Wood is probably named after a grant of land to a monastic foundation. In 1327 the area was known as le Monkeswode, derived from the Old English *munuc* and *wudu*, a 'monk's wood, grove or forest'. The wood is a remnant of the ancient forests which covered much of this part of Britain through forgotten millennia.

The western edge of the wood is formed by the north–south flowing Lee Brook. Rising in Kitchen Wood by Dronfield Woodhouse, it flows through Cowley Bottom and School Wood (a glade of campion bank and wayfarer's tree), under Lee Bridge, through the deep, dank, toad-flax-heart of Broombank Plantation to the second, bigger Lee Bridge. Why two Lee Bridges within the space of a mile? The name was Lee Brygge in 1586 and is derived from the Old English *leah* and *brycg*, 'the bridge in the clearing in a wood'. The upper bridge is scarcely noticed as you go along the road from Dronfield to Peakley Hill but from the woodland on either hand the high, rather graceful arch is seen to advantage. The present bridge was built in 1841, designed by G. Davidson, then the County Architect.

The lower Lee Bridge is set peacefully where the Barlow Brook runs by high banks, meadows on either side, just west of the Monk Wood. It seems very much as if it were erected for packhorse traffic.

If you look south-westwards from Roughpiece Wood you will see the 488 feet (148 metre) high knob which is really the run-out of the spur dropping from Bole Hill. The wood that clothes its northern slope is called Cobnar, 'Cobbenouere' in 1324. The name is the Old English term for a slope or ridge. This is very fitting for it is, in fact, a wood on a ridge or slope. The trees of Cobnar Wood are very old and there is little doubt that the farmland stretching from the brook up to Monk Wood Farm (the most recent part of which was built in 1735) was once forested, making Cobnar and Monk Woods one, a remnant of the older forest lands hereabouts.

Upon the broad shoulder dropping into the valley from Grange Hill and Bole Hill stand the two largest settlements, Barlow and Barlow Common Side. 'Barleie' in Domesday Book, the name has undergone many changes including 'Baalega' and 'Berlegh'. The name seems to be a derivation of either the Old English words *bar* and *leah*, a 'clearing where barley grew'; though it has been suggested that the word 'barley' was derived from the Barleys of Barley in Lancashire, a well-known family in the area in ancient times. In the church at Barlow is the tomb of Robert Barley, 1464. His influence spread throughout the valley, if we allow that Barlow obtained its name from the Barleys. The name Brierley (Wood and Farm) is doubtless obtained from a corruption of Barlow and Barley. G.H.B. Ward, 'king of ramblers' and rural scholar, refers to this in the following observation: '...there is no district which illustrates more clearly than this valley the permanence of names with slightly disguising phonetic changes'.

Barlow village is a small, tree-populated place with an old wood-towered church, farms, an inn and a famous annual well-dressing ceremony; Common Side is a child, a drab, hard-working child, an upstart above a narrowing in the valley floor. The place grew up due to local working of coal seams in the carboniferous coal measures forming the surface of this part of Derbyshire in the nineteenth century.

Looking out over the valley it is possible to see the reasons for Common Side's development, the remains of many small collieries. There are still the old mines near Cowley Bottom, the old 'footrill' near upper Lee Bridge, the ruins along Sud Brook and Barlow Brook, and the romantic mine above Broombank Plantation. I can well remember the enticing red finger of that tottering chimney through a deep canopy of holly and sycamore. Now the remains are pit waste and heaped bricks, the shadow of former woodland activities. But Rutland Terrace and Common Side remain across the brook.

From the wooded recesses of the valley floor let us take the hill paths and sky-ways above. Bole Hill is 700 feet (213 metres) above the sea, a well-defined knoll overlooking the vale from the south. Sheltering beneath the summit copse (surprisingly vigorous despite the exposure) is a fine old house, a private academy at the latter end of the nineteenth century. The name derives from the Middle English *bole*, a place where ore was smelted before the days of furnaces, often (as here) in a round cavity on a high hill top. Carboniferous iron ores were doubtless extracted locally and drawn to the top of this eminence.

Two miles (3.2 km) along the gradually ascending ridge to the west the summit of Grange Hill is reached, almost a thousand feet above the sea – a place where 'wind and sky join on earth's round brim'.

Grangehouse and Highashes Farms stand guardian on the southern side of Grange Lane, between Bole Hill and Grange Hill. Barlow Grange is an aged hamlet of farms which it is easy to imagine fortified at one period. Barlow Grange was known as Barley Grange in 1306, originally a granary and later an outlying farm where crops were stored belonging to the feudal lord of Barlow. By Grange Hall Farm was a moat-like pond, and sycamores lean to the east, trees of great age.

Doubling back upon the direction from Bole Hill to Barlow Grange is a long, smooth ridge dropping to Cutthorpe Common End, almost 3 miles (4.75 km) eastwards from Grange Hill. Along the ridge are Overgreen, Ingmanthorpe and Pratthall, farming hamlets seen from a good distance due to their open situation. To the south is the wooded recess of the Linacre Valley, enchanting with daffodil and gorse in spring, the reservoir surface reflecting the sky through the encircling trees. At the head of the Linacre Valley is the steep, rough country drained by Birley Brook – a delightful place, out of the reach of the strong winds which howl over Grange Hill not far away. But this is not strictly in the area of Barlow Vale. Between the two ridges rising to Grange Hill is the steep-sided field-filled hollow drained by Sud Brook, which joins Barlow Brook near the mouth of the Vale.

Oxton Rakes is the name given to the collection of cottages and farms nestling in the upper reach of this sub-vale. The banks of the brook are packed with trees, old and lovely. And the situation of Oxton Rakes is magically Mozartian – 'ox paths' in a green hollow.

Running roughly parallel with Sud Brook to the north is the little stream which courses down the narrow depression backing Crowhole. The stream is born in the high pastures behind Spitewinter Farm and descends by woody way and impounding wall for 600 feet (183 metres) to the meanders where Dunston Brook becomes Barlow Brook. In the upper reaches of this side valley are two ancient farms, Grangewood and Grangelumb, pleasantly sited among trees below the raging plateau-land hard by. They both enjoy wide views of the lower Barlow Vale and beyond to the industrial, yet seemingly green, east. Grangewood is a logical enough name for the trees around are the nearest to Barlow Grange. The 'lumb' in Grangelumb is a derivation from the Old English *lum,* a pool. There seems to be no trace of a pool now but this omission is counteracted a little lower down; here is Crowhole Reservoir. This part of our country seems short of expanses of water, always a focal point of country wandering. Here the artificiality of the earthen bank is largely lost and refreshing views can be had from the fields on either hand, glimpses down through green and branch to the ripples of deep water.

Below the reservoir and the old lane which dips to the valley and rises south-westwards to Muckspout Farm and Wilday Green is a wooden footbridge across the stream, by gorsey banks and the old, twisted oak. Here I have spent many sunlit hours, playing by the water or swinging from the branches. What peace there is in forgotten dells.

Quarter of a mile (0.5 km) below the footbridge are the remains of yet another small colliery, more evidence that our locality is built up of carboniferous coal measures, some holding productive coal seams. In less than ¾ mile (1.2 km) the stream flows beneath low arches at

Crowhole and joins the mother where she meanders at the narrowing of the main vale. The name of this little hamlet of farms and ancient cottages has undergone numerous changes in the last three and a half centuries: Skroholl at the 1610 Survey and Crowhole in 1630. The sprawling Common Side, greedy child that it seems to be, has taken in Crowhole to an alarming degree so that its identity is hard to ascertain at a swift passage. So much for local planning.

Along the spur which falls from the western moorland north-west of Barlow Grange runs the long, straight procession of Rumbling Street, a lane probably of Roman origin. Who else but the Romans could site their routes along such geometrically perfect lines? It is a climbing, sweeping road along the ridge's crest and leads onto the open top beyond. The title was presumably given as a result of heavy usage and consequent 'rumblings' of traffic in medieval times. Up Rumbling Street are numerous old holdings, easily seen from the valley floor: Ridgeway House (self-explanatory), Meanfield (originally *mëne feld*, the Old English term for a stony piece of common pasture or cultivated land), and the sky-facing hamlet of Moorhall, the place of origin of the Foljambes. Morehowsse in 1563, the place had become Morehall twenty years later, as recorded in the Hardwick Charters at Chatsworth House.

Here, where the old road curves up onto the level pastures moorward, the fields look more to the sky than across to the quilted pattern of man's cultivations on the far side of the vale. There are not many trees around Moorhall, understandably; just a handful of rowans and wind-bent hawthorn.

Footpaths radiate northwards from Moorhall (what a romantic, image-conjuring name it is) and all soon swing down the slopes. The whole of the land on the northern side of Rumbling Street fans out and drops gracefully in copsed folds. This is a north-facing slope where a galaxy of woods, large and small, fall to the river meadows by Cordwell, Millthorpe and Bradley Lane. Each is as individualistic in character as its ancient name suggests.

Hollin Wood fills the defile through which a nameless stream runs by Barlow Woodseats. Hollin is the modern derivation of *holegn*, the Old English form for 'holly', though there are as many deciduous trees as hollies here nowadays. Barlow Woodseats itself is a great farm, perched high above the stream and out of the wood on a level shoulder of grassland. The present building dates from the sixteenth century though there has been a house here since at least 1269, when Barlewodsetes referred to a 'house in the wood belonging to Barlow' (*setes* and *sëte* being the Old English equivalents for 'house').

Here lived the Mowers, famous in the vale for a long period and worthy locals, leaving copious records. Robert Mower gave the profits of 'two closes', called Maggeth Lees, for the instruction of ten children in 1719. Prudence Mower donated £60 towards the erecting of a school and augmenting the master's salary in 1725. The name Mower is still well known hereabouts and spoken of highly.

A short step down the lane from Barlow Woodseats is Johnnygate Farm, 'Jony gate' in 1563, the 'gate' originating as *geat*, a hole or gap; no doubt the entrance to the Barlow Woodseats property was here in olden times. Across two fields to the south of Johnnygate Farm is Sweetingsick Wood, a small, mixed deciduous stand getting its charming name from the fact that a small stream flows lazily over the very gentle slope, *sic* meaning a flat stream, especially one in flat marshland. Sweeting was probably a farmer or landowner.

Harker Wood is across three more fields to the south-east, taking its name from one William Harker, according to S. Glover in his *Directory of the County of Derby* published in 1829. A small rill flows through this wood and where the Sweetingsick and Harker streams join is Dobmeadow Wood, a magic wood if ever I saw one. Here the very light is charged beneath the ancient canopy, the birds are silent and the fungi more riotously hued than anywhere else in the vicinity. The very name seems to confirm this, for though one authority suggests that 'Dob' is from 'Rob', a shortened form of Robert (hence probably the wood by Robert Mower's meadow), I prefer the explanation of John Derry and G.H.B. Ward that 'Dob' probably comes from the Middle English *hob,* a hobgoblin or a fairy. Yes, this is truly a wood by a Fairy Meadow, with sun-drenched views down to the military line of Lombardy poplars striding along the roadside by Bradley Lane Farm.

From Moorhall you can take the northward path that soon drops into the valley of the Pingle Dike, joining Millthorpe Brook a little way eastwards of Millthorpe village. The path descends steeply in places and at night presents an interesting expedition, either uphill or down, though the lights of Cordwell and Millthorpe help on the descent in winter, when most of the trees are naked. This upper part of the wood is called Moorhall Wood while, across the stream, to the left as you goes down, is Meekfields Wood and the path soon takes you through Rose Wood (perhaps from *raw*, rows of trees, referring to the fact that most of this is plantation), three names though really one big wood, best seen from the hilltops around Holmesfield. The path swings round to the left through fields and brings you out by the stream at Millthorpe.

I have heard tell of a certain old Moorhall farmer who used this path almost nightly, the quicker to reach the inn at Millthorpe. He would regularly return up the wood totally inebriated, bellowing and threshing tree trunks that got in his uncertain way with his stick. More than one frightened walker fled from his path, and his roars were often heard by local folk at Cordwell.

From Moorhall yet another path strikes to the north-west, a high field-path this time crossing the Meek Fields before reaching Unthank Lane. Up here you are on top of the local world and every breeze beneath the clouds is felt. There is always the wide view northwards and eastwards here, deep wooded valley trough and rolling, quilted hillside. Across there, 2 miles (3.25 km) away, is the church-capped hill of Holmesfield, and to the left the distant suggestions of Lodge Moor beyond Sheffield, 10 miles (16 km) away. On clear days it is an easy task to pick out Bolsover Castle perched upon its Permian limestone escarpment away below the eastern sky, glinting. Dronfield's highest outskirts peep through wooded angles of hills 4½ miles (7.2 km) to the north-east as the crow flies. The lapwings wheel and curlews call. This is the land of youth, where every line of distant fracto-cumulus reminds us of childhood dreams in a summer sky.

Millthorpe consists of a mixture of dwellings, ancient cottages and farms on the one hand and a suburban overflow on the other. Old Millthorpe is set off the main road and down by the picturesque ford through the main brook. The most interesting building in the settlement was undoubtedly the ancient mill, now swept away. A small weir on the brook half a mile upstream by Cordwell fed a race which turned the wheels to grind local corn, indicative of the long-established arable farming pattern in the district. Thomas Bunting of Millthorpe was the miller 150 years ago but the business changed hands many times before the mill was closed a few years ago, when the Haslams of Fox Lane had the business. The meaning of the village's name is quite obvious –

'Milnthorpe' in 1487, the world originates from the Old English *myln*, a mill, and the Old East Scandinavian *porp*, a secondary settlement or outlying hamlet.

The charm of this leafy corner has all but gone. There is now a rash of new houses where the old mill once stood above the ford.

But now a backward glance – to the slopes facing south over the vale from Millthorpe to Monk Wood. Here the contours produce a smooth, swelling drop of 400 feet (123 metres) from the hill-crown at Cartledge. Little and Great Brind Woods stand around the 500 foot (154 metre) contour; uncrossed by public footpaths they are little known. Perhaps the name originated as 'le Brynde', recorded in 1457, and meaning 'burnt wood'. Below the woods lie the wood pigeon filled acres that reach the ancient land from Johnnygate cross-roads to Brindwoodgate. On this lane is Highlightley Farm, a beautiful old place with fine gardens and a terrace overlooking the river meadow below. Here lived Miss Winifred Wilson, notable landscape artist and horse-woman. Miss Wilson was one of the well-known vale family of Wilson. Her quaint former home is matched by its old name. Five hundred years ago it was 'Heghelyghtley', originating from the Old English form *leoht leah*, to which was prefixed *heah*; literally 'the high, bright woodland clearing', appreciated if you stand on Rumbling Street at about 600 feet (184 metres) and look over Dobmeadow Wood to Great Brind Wood; there, in what seems little more than a clearing high above the brook, stands Highlightley, catching the shafts of sun as they strike from the south.

A path leads up and over the fields behind the farm and reaches Peakley Hill in 1 mile (1.5 km). From various vantage points hereabouts are wonderful vistas of the middle and upper valley, while below is the hamlet of Brindwoodgate, 'the opening or entrance to the burnt wood'. John Derry describes the views from Peakley Hill:

> 'In front the open swell of Ramsley Moor breaks the fall of the breezy brown moor into the green and cultivated seclusion of the valley. It is a very graceful scene of pasture and woodland, at which the moors peer over with their reminder of wilderness'.

Looking back up the steep hill above the Brind Woods to the north-west can be seen the cluster of farms forming Cartledge. The pride of this hamlet is the hall, a low-built structure of late Elizabethan times on the site of a much more ancient house occupied by John Wolstenholme in the fifteenth century. The magnificent oak beams and panelling and the fine plaster mouldings in the lounge and main bedroom are well worth seeing. An ancient carved text has lately been restored and placed over the lounge fireplace, a relic of Attercliffe Hall, now demolished. The settlement occupies the top of that conspicuous spur which extends southwards from Holmesfield out and down valley-wards. The top of the spur is 800 feet (246 metres) above the sea and not far away a spring gives birth to a tributary of Millthorpe Brook. It is the proximity of this tributary that gives the place its unusual name. *Kartr* is the Old Norse word for rough, stony ground, and *laec* is the Old English term for the stream; by 1328 the name had become 'Cartelache', a 'slow stream in rough, common land'. The Gilchrists lived at Cartledge Hall, spell-bound by the magic of the vale at their feet; yes, the views of the upper and lower valley are unforgettable from the Cartledge spur.

Five hundred yards northwards along the lane is Holmesfield, perhaps 'Holm's open country' or, according to Ekwall, 'holm' may have the same sense of 'hill' as in the Old Saxon; anyhow, here is sited the hill-top village – Holmesfelt in 1086, Hulmesfeld in 1331 and Hownefeld by 1546. The village was owned by the Deincourts from 1066 until the reign of Edward II.

Saint Swithin's square-towered church stands at the top of the knob around which the village is built, at a little more than 850 feet (259 metres) above the sea. The church is one of the most conspicuous in Britain and, what is more, moving due east from the hill top, higher land is not reached for more than 1500 miles (2400 km), upon reaching the Central Russian Heights, 100 miles (160 km) south-east of Moscow – there is not a church situated as high as Holmesfield's until Roslavl, looking down upon the lowlands of White Russia.

It is interesting to note that the village seemed to be the centre of the agriculture of the upper vale even 150 years ago, as today. In 1846 there were two blacksmiths, four horse-nail manufacturers, two saw-handle manufacturers, three scythe makers and two wheelwrights in Holmesfield; no fewer than four of these craftsmen being Biggins, an old family hereabouts and still farming in the upper vale.

From the fields at the end of Cartledge lane a wide view of the upper vale is had, unsurpassed in Derbyshire for variety of contour and colour.

Looking south-westwards is a rectangle of land deep in mystic charm, from Holmesfield to Owler Bar, to the moors above Smeekley, to the already familiar fields about Moorhall. This is the last old corner to explore; and what a wealth of history is hidden by the ancient yews and beeches and the old stone slabs beneath leaning stacks.

Descending the smooth farmland slopes from Holmesfield Common to the deep upper-valley floor is Horsleygate Lane, alternately hedged with hawthorn and high walled.

Halfway down this slant-wise lane is the ancient front of Horsleygate Old Hall, former home of the Lowe family. The Wolstenholmes lived here up to 1814, when they moved further up the lane. The buildings are very old and the Norman-type arch by the house is indeed unusual in these parts. Less than ½ mile (0.75 km) further down is Horsleygate, where the Wolstenholmes were living 500 years ago. Named from the family of Adam de Horsley in about 1388, the name had taken its present form by 1494. The place was probably one of the gates of Holmesfield Park, Horseley's gate to the Park. The old house has been added to in the last two centuries and was the home of the hunting Wilsons for many years.

Below Horsleygate Lane, down the fields, is the hamlet of Cordwell. Grimsell Lane drops steeply to Millthorpe from the lane, part of an old trackway (possibly Roman) which ran northwards from Rumbling Street, through the valley and over towards Sheffield. The lane gets its name from the 'Grimsells', three closes. Its existence is not common knowledge for it is largely overgrown and a water-course in wet weather.

Cordwell is undoubtedly the development of 'Coldewell' in an attempt to represent scribally a dialect pronunciation for 'cold'. Anyway, the Printed Derbyshire Subsidy Rolls of 1902, 1908 and 1922 show the Coldewell was the name in 1328. If the 'cold well' that tradition sites by Eweford Bridge, where local people used to get water, is the reason for the place's name then others argue that there have been Caldwells and Caudwells living in the vicinity for nearly half a millennium; Thomas Caudwell appears in the Holmesfield Court Roll of 1489 and there were Caudwells living at Moorhall until very recently. There is quite a possibility that this sector of the vale gets its name from a great local family; then again, there is the ice-cold well by the bridge.

Cordwell Farm is probably the third house built on the site of very ancient Cordwell Hall. The present house is in two distinct styles, an older rear portion with low, mullioned windows looking out over a fine farmyard, and the newer front (about 1790) looking onto the delightful yew-shadowed garden. Many are the times I have watched great thunder clouds gathering over Moorhall and the head of the valley from the stack yard, filled with newly thatched corn and haystacks. The Key family have farmed here for a long time, yeomen farmers of the old order. Now, through marriage, the Biggins are there – two old vale families linked and farming in one of Derbyshire's most delightful corners.

Along the road towards Millthorpe is Carpenter House, the home of author and philosopher Edward Carpenter almost until his death in 1929, a great friend of William Key of Cordwell.

The road through the valley crossed Millthorpe Brook by a ford, where the shepherds drove their flocks, hence 'Eweford'. In 1834 a bridge was built, one of the most graceful of local stone bridges, taking the name of the ford. Yews stand by the bridge; the valleys of the district have been yew-clad for a thousand years or more – like the yews of Hope Valley, tradition asserts that these helped to make the bows used at Agincourt.

Immediately over the brook the little lane on the left leads up the twisting way for over 400 feet (122 metres) to the level sky-ways about Moorhall. This is Unthank Lane, and what a name in historical association! The antiquarian Addy had it that the name 'Unthank' comes to us from the dim shadows of primeval nature worship – 'the shout of congratulation which announced that the oracles had spoken'. Whatever its uncertain origin, we can be sure that the name is linked with the Old English term *unpanc*, meaning 'ill-will', land held 'against the will' – a squatter's holding; that is, land claimed and built upon without the lord of the community of free-holder's consent. Another authority believes that the name originated from the amalgamation of a personal name, 'Hun', and *thwong*, referring to Hun's land measured out with a thong of leather. Whichever is the origin of this unusual name we can be sure that Unthank Hall is extremely old. Over a century ago a local newspaper correspondent fell out with the owners of Unthank Hall and subsequently referred to the place in his writings derisively as 'Nut Thank Hall'. The name underwent various changes and is found as 'Nut Bank' in Bagshaw's *History, Gazetteer and Directory of Derbyshire*, published in 1846!

The Lowes have been in residence for centuries and an earlier member of the family planted many beech trees on his land, now fine specimens, breaking the winds that howl on winter nights straight down off the south-western moors. The defile below the hall contains pretty Burrs Wood, the haunt of turtle doves and badgers and carpeted with bluebell and edged with lady's smock in spring.

Just as a Regency gazebo leads the eye towards a focal point down an avenue or flagged path, so the symmetry of Smeekley Wood acts upon the senses and balances the sweep of valley side when looking up the vale from Peakley Hill or Dunston or Cartledge.

Smeekley is a gargantuan hump rising as a perfect dome (an ideal site for Stone Age fortification you would think) and now conifer-clad. In the Holmesfield Manor Roll of 1364 this was Smeclif, originating from the Old English *smede* (smooth) with the common development of *clif* to *ley,* hence 'the smooth or bare cliff'. Unfortunately much of this verdant upper corner of Barlow Vale is forbidden territory, private estate; but how magical and much more enticing when we see down through a dark, secret tilt of woodland where we should not go! The main stream bends round to the south of Smeekley Wood, taking a final south-westerly course.

To reach the upper end of the vale, 'the very fount of youth on high and howling plain', you must take the steep hill after crossing Eweford Bridge in Cordwell Bottom.

This is Fox Lane, named after a local family who figure prominently in the Holmesfield Manor Rolls from 1481 until 1586, John Fox being referred to as resident at Fox Lane Farm in 1498. The present farm dates only from 1691, four-square and mullion-windowed where the lane levels out onto the moor. If the front of the house is examined the markings, probably referring to a Mower, will be seen quite clearly. Lower down the lane is Bank Green Farm, to my mind the best-situated house in the county. The ancient farm, home of the numerous Helliwells who still populate the vicinity, is now totally derelict but well worth looking at on its hillside knob, a position so naturally fortified that I cannot believe that the present house, probably late sixteenth century, is the first to occupy the site. It can be seen from miles around and from it there are uninterrupted views to every point of the compass, most of the features mentioned in this chapter being plainly visible on a clear day.

And now, up onto the level moorland road where the Don and the Derwent have their water-parting. High on this level brown land are two crosses, the famous Fox Lane crosses. The one to the north-west of the road is the more conspicuous, standing on the moor and brushed by waving nardus and molinia grasses and carved 'Here lies Godfrey'; not a lost traveller in dim days of old but a young Fox Lane lad, Godfrey Silcock, about 1890. The other cross is in better order and stands in the young pine plantation on the left hand, originally marking the old bridleway.

Half a mile beyond Fox Lane Farm the lane joins old Rumbling Street, not hawthorn-edged now but straight as a die across the moor and stone walled. Across Rumbling Street is Leash Fen, over 500 acres in area and nearly 1000 feet (305 metres) above the sea. *Lë c fenn* is the Old English for 'boggy marshland'. But the Leyches owned Coldewell and the old legend has it that:

> *When Leech-field was a market town,*
> *Chesterfield was gorse and broom.*
> *Now Chesterfield's a market town,*
> *Leech-field a marsh is grown.*

Looking back from the old cross on the molinia-level by Fox Lane, looking back and across to cloud castles tinted yellow by the late afternoon sunshine, the whole eastern world opens up as far as the Permian escarpment under Bolsover and its castle.

At the feet the young brook, the heart of the glorious vale through which you have travelled, is chasing by tormentil-bank and rush-bed. Soon it will be swelling by dairy meadows, heavy with the smell of wet hides and lime fruits, but up here this child of the peaty marsh reminds us of those other childhood dream days in the deep woods, by butterburr banks far away in the valley below, under a still evening sky. Silence and a still, blue sky.

WALK 1

Dronfield to Linacre and the Return

Outline:	**Cowley, Highlightley, Moorhall, Barlow Grange, Linacre Reservoirs, Ingmanthorpe, Wilday Green, Peakley Hill and Cowley**
Map:	**OS 1:25,000 Pathfinder Sheet 761 (SK27/37)**
Distance:	**14 miles/22.5 km**
Parking:	**Dronfield Civic Centre or railway station**

Route

Leave **Dronfield** Civic Centre and climb the steep road to the south – Farwater Lane (so called because the residents of the Holborn area of the town fetched water from a spring at the bottom of the slope) – and turn left up Gosforth Lane to the Hyde Park Inn on the top of the hill.

Cross the Unstone–Dronfield bypass (A61) and turn right along Cowley Lane. In ¼ mile (0.5 km) the lane turns down the slope to the left but you go ahead, along the farm drive to Hills Farm. A path continues west beyond the farm; at the end of the next field turn right then left to skirt the ivy-covered ruins of Sload's House. Cut across behind this ruin and down the fields to cross a small stream which rises on the right in Spring Wood. Cowley was called College in 1315, a place in a wood or clearing where charcoal was burnt.

After crossing two more fields on the upward slope the lane from Cowley Bar to Cowley is reached. Here, on the roadside, is Cowley Hall and a row of very ancient cottages (map reference: 333/774). Cross the road and the path leads straight down and across two brooks, with a rise of 30 feet (9 metres) between them.

The next field is irregularly shaped but the path will not be lost if you bear left, aiming for the farthest corner.

Once through the hedge look for a path leading off leftwards; follow this and soon the old road connecting Holmesfield and Barlow will be joined, deep-set and overgrown. In 600 yards (549 metres) turn right

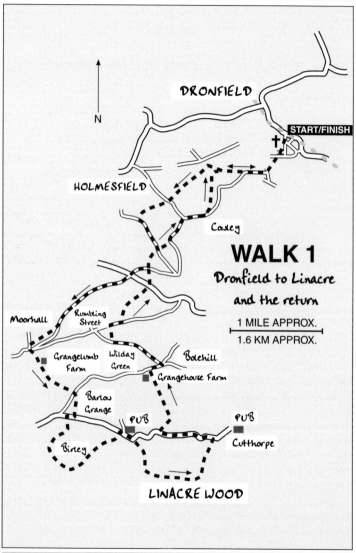

N

DRONFIELD

START/FINISH

HOLMESFIELD

Caxtey

WALK 1
Dronfield to Linacre
and the return

1 MILE APPROX.

1.6 KM APPROX.

Moorhall

Rumbling
Street

Grangelumb
Farm

Wilday
Green

Bolehill

Grangehouse Farm

Barlow
Grange

PUB

PUB

Cutthorpe

Birley

LINACRE WOOD

into a pasture field and the roof of Highlightley Farm will be seen, former home of Miss Winifred Wilson, artist and horsewoman.

Robert Barley of Barley was the first husband of Bess of Hardwick and his family have left their name in many places hereabouts: Brierley Wood above Unstone Green, Barlow Brook, the many Barlows (including Barlow Woodseats) and the corruption to Birley, the old farm we pass later, above Linacre Reservoirs.

Cross the B6051 road, taking the lane up past Johnnygate Farm and the fine old Tudor hall of Barlow Woodseats. From there the ancient trackway leading up the north-facing valley offers a better route in wet weather, reaching Moorhall in ¾ mile (1.25 km). Alternatively take the stile on the left just beyond the hall and follow this by its winding gorse-bush way, cross the track already mentioned and cut up the fields directly to Moorhall. A little way before reaching the hamlet an unusual stile is climbed; stones set in the wall between two gateposts allow you to pass on top of the wall and down its end into the next field.

Moorhall is a grand little settlement standing at 850 feet (259 metres) which looks down the long, smooth spur towards the Barlow Vale. The place can be extremely bleak, being set on the edge of an area which has a winter as 'continental' in severity as anywhere in the British Isles.

Taking the path south-east past Grangewood and **Grangelumb** farms the sylvan dell containing the Wilday Brook is crossed. After the open fields on the edge of the moors this is a place of great charm, overhung by ash and willow and beech, and hazy blue with bells in May.

Cross Grange Lane and pass through the farms which make up **Barlow Grange**, with the duck pond behind an ancient barn. Six hundred years ago this was Barley Grange, a granary (later an outlying farm) where crops belonging to the lord of the manor of Barlow were stored.

After a short climb the lane joins the Cutthorpe–Baslow road (B6050) and turning right for 200 yards (182 metres) the private road (public path only) to Birley Grange is followed on the left. In 1154 this was a *Byre leah*, or 'farm in a clearing'. A few yards beyond this junction is a triangulation station, standing at 980 feet (298 metres) above the sea.

In less than ½ mile (0.75 km) along the lane the infant Birley Brook is reached, at a sharp bend of the track. Follow this brook down through gorse and, in early April, along banks covered with wild daffodils.

Bluebells follow in their turn and make the walk memorable. Take a footpath to the left where it crosses the brook (map reference: 318/728). After a steady rise to Cowclose Farm you reach Overgreen. Here you can shorten the walk by going down the lane by Piker Storth Farm, by Oxton Rakes to Wilday Green, otherwise continue south-east to Pratthall village, bearing right in the village and down the lane for 100 yards (80 metres) before taking a path cutting down to Linacre Reservoirs on the right. Follow this path through the woods of sycamore and spruce not far above the water's edge – more like 'the lilaced Danubian shore' than a Derbyshire reservoir bank!

Linacre is an unusual name hereabouts and is derived from the Old English terms for flax, line, and a plot of arable land, 'aecer'. Hence, 'lineacer', literally 'cultivated land where flax was grown'. By 1189 the original designation had become 'Lynacra' and this underwent numerous changes before becoming the modern 'Linacre'.

When opposite the impounding wall of the lowest of the three reservoirs take a path north through the larches of Kitchen-flat Wood, brilliant in their new raiment in spring. Once on the B6050 road walk west to Ingmanthorpe (Ingman's *thorp*, or outlying farm) and here take one of the footpaths leading off to Oxton Rakes, crossing the tree-lined Sud Brook by a footbridge (map reference: 332/738). Continue on through **Wilday Green** beyond the top of the next ridge. When almost at the base of the

Linacre Middle Reservoir

wall of Crowhole Reservoir (just past Muckspout Farm) take the path to the right up to Rumbling Street Farm. This lovely little path crosses the Crowhole Stream by a pretty footbridge. An old oak guards the farther bank and a lime leans streamwards to the right.

On both trees and footbridge handrail you can pick out names of local boys, carved long ago. The late Frank Needham remembers how the Wilday Green boys spent many happy hours here, playing in the trees and clearing gorse bushes so that they could play cricket on the level ground by the brook. You can still see the old stone roller that they dragged with chains from Barlow Woodseats to roll the 'pitch'. It lies half-buried with foliage a little way below the footbridge.

Turn right down the street (of Roman origin) for 200 yards (180 metres) and turn left, down through the fields on the edge of Dobmeadow (Fairymeadow) Wood and cross Bradley Lane and Dunston Brook, up the big field to join the lane a little way east of Highlightley Farm. This is familiar territory and the path is followed up the fields to Peakley Hill. On joining the road (map reference: 334/766) bear left up the hill and turn right at the junction, through **Cowley** village. Just beyond Cowley Mission, a small stone and slate chapel built in 1893, go through a squeezer stile on the left (map reference: 339/771). Go across the fields, bearing right in ½ mile (0.75 km) past the front of Hills Farm, then go back along the drive to Cowley Lane and so return by way of the Unstone–Dronfield bypass (A61) bridge and down Gosforth Lane to **Dronfield** Town Centre.

WALK 2

Seven Holmesfield Halls

Outline:	**Holmesfield, Cartledge, Cordwell, Unthank, Bank Green, Horsleygate, Lidgate, Fanshawe Gate, Holmesfield**
Map:	**OS: 1:25,000 Pathfinder Sheet 761 (SK27/37)**
Distance:	**6½ miles/10.4 km**
Parking:	**Holmesfield church car park**

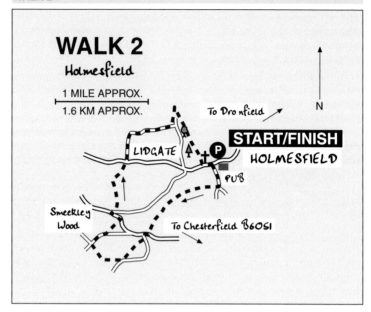

WALK 2

Holmesfield

1 MILE APPROX.
1.6 KM APPROX.

To Dronfield

N

LIDGATE

START/FINISH
HOLMESFIELD

PUB

Smeekley Wood

To Chesterfield B6051

Route

Holmesfield church stands conspicuously at 860 feet (262 metres) above sea level, on the highest ground in the village, surveying its parish. From the church walk 150 yards (135 metres) down the road towards Dronfield Woodhouse and Sheffield and turn right at the village green, along Cartledge Lane. At the end of the lane is the hamlet of Cartledge, on a spur overlooking the broad green angles of Barlow Vale. Before turning right down Millthorpe Lane look at the low-gabled house on the left, behind a high wall.

This is the famous Cartledge Hall, one of the oldest houses in this part of Derbyshire and rescued from near-dereliction by the Doncasters after World War II. The house was completely rebuilt in the reign of Elizabeth I, on the site of an older house occupied by John Wolstenholme in the fifteenth century. The plaster mouldings are perhaps the pride of Cartledge, similar to those at demolished Greenhill Hall and at Unthank Hall and Barlow Woodseats Hall.

Turning right down Millthorpe Lane for a few yards take the path (right). The first field is pasture and slopes steeply towards Cordwell Valley, a grand field for sledging on winter days of crisp snow. From the top of the field most of the upper Barlow Vale opens before the beholder; woods and winding hedges, deep summer green or grey angle of winter hill. And buried in odd corners are the houses of another age, homes and centres of life for solid yeomen for centuries. Let us find some of them.

At the bottom of the steep sledging field cross five fields, keeping roughly on the same contour. At the far side of the sixth field after leaving Millthorpe Lane a footbridge crosses what seems to be a stream-bed in dry weather, or a rushing torrent after rain. This is Grimsell Lane, part of an old trackway (possibly Roman, possibly ancient British) which runs north from Rumbling Street on the southern side of the vale and over the Holmesfield ridge towards the Sheaf Valley. Go on now, across two more fields and make down to a stone stile in the far corner of the third field.

The view to the valley floor is wide once more; Cordwell Farm stands directly at the bottom of the slope and the next field, the 'Cliff', is part of that farm (so called because of the steep slope on the western side overlooking a bouncing brook). Go down the 'Cliff' to a footbridge and leaning sycamores where my great grandfather cut his initials long ago. Here is a cross-roads of footpaths (map reference: 313/768); one path to Millthorpe, one forward to Cordwell Bottom and another up steps to Horsleygate Lane. You can make a detour here, up right, to look at the second hall. Up one steep pasture field you come to Horsleygate Lane, a very ancient route-way leading from the valley to Holmesfield.

A few yards down the lane, on the right, is Horsleygate Old Hall, home of the Lowes since the Wolstenholmes moved to Horsleygate Farm (nearer Holmesfield) in 1814. The old mullions are worthy of note and so is the narrow arch beside the house, reminiscent of Norman times. The last Lowe died in 1965.

Back now, down the field and right, across three more, to the road at Cordwell Bottom (map reference: 311/765). The path comes down onto the road by a flight of steep steps by the site of the former Mission building and just down past this is Eweford Bridge, built in 1834 to replace the original ford beneath great yews. Take the left-hand turn after crossing the bridge, signposted 'Unthank'. A few yards beyond the turn a footpath leads off on the right up the fields to Unthank Hall. You are now in the Peak National Park, having crossed the boundary on step-ping over the stile from Unthank Lane. This lane forms the Park boundary right up to its junction with Rumbling Street on the moors.

Unthank Hall is a magnificent old house in a well-sheltered position under an angle of southern hill with views down the valley to the east. There is a conglomeration of wings to the Hall, bits added at different times. But the oldest part is that nearest the lane. In an upper room is some fine plaster moulding and the ancient stables at the entrance to the farmyard was probably once the private chapel. At the top of the spacious yard is a well-preserved cruck barn dating maybe from about AD1400 (cruck barn takes its name from the great crucks or beams supporting the roof and were originally the work of the Angles, who were skilled in wood-craft, coming as they did from a low-lying forested area and utilising the great deciduous forests of this part of Mercia). The barn has a frame which cannot fall down – made with only four tools – and was covered with daub and wattle and had a thatched roof, serving as home for the farming family, their animals and implements.

More recently, when the hall was built close by to accommodate the farming family, the barn was built up in stone – as we see so many still – the same timber frame serving as the major structure. Hence the great cruck barns of Cartledge, Unthank and in other corners throughout our part of the country may be more than 600 years old. The Lowes of Unthank have looked after their precious heritage and the present owner's great-grandfather set the fine stands of beech that now grace the property.

Above the Hall is the stack-yard and opposite the stack-yard gate into Unthank Lane is a stile. Climb this and cross down the pasture to a line of beeches and another stile (map reference: 305/761). A remark-able little wood is now entered, occupying a steep west-facing slope. In spring the floor is a mass of gold as the naturalised daffodil buds open. Later bluebells form a blue fall against the white and green of newly-burst birch, and still later rhododendrons bank rosily up to scots pines among the beech when cuckoos call. A footbridge takes you across Burrs Stream and out of the wood into marshy ground where the path ahead is indistinct. Look for lady's smock here.

Make a line directly at right-angles to the stream, up the broken slope to Knowles Farm. Keep to the right of the farm and when the first

Barlow Commonside from Cartledge (Barlow Vale)

November snow: Holmesfield from Moorhall (Barlow Vale)

Linacre Reservoir (Walk 1)

Autumn in upper Derwent Dale (Walk 5)

Abbey Brook Clough (Walk 8)

Bleaklow and Oyster Clough from Blackden Edge (Walk 7)

Billingham Library

Tel: 01642 528084

billingham library@stockton gov.uk

Borrowed Items 23/10/2017 11:58

XXXXXX5714

Item Title	Due Date
* Walking in Peakland	13/11/2017
* Haynes carp fishing manual : the step-by-step guide to becoming a better car	13/11/2017

* Indicates items borrowed today
Thank you for using self service
Please reply to your voter information letter
Delays waste money you have to do it by law.

Opening hours:
Mon, Tues: 8.30am - 7.00pm
Wed, Thur, Fri: 8.30am - 5.00pm
Sat: 9.30am - 4.00pm

buildings are reached drop, again at right angles, towards another stream. Cross this morass (map reference: 302/761) and climb the pasture field ahead to Fox Lane.

Like Unthank Lane, Fox Lane is of great antiquity. A thousand years ago it would have taken men and livestock up the valley-side from the impenetrable dense woodland in the vale-bottom to the open pastures of the hilltops around Leash Fen, once a thriving settlement and now waste marsh and heather moor at 950 feet (290 metres).

High up on a knob the sad remnants of Bank Green Farm stand as a testament to the intentional neglect of a historic property in the interests of fox hunting. From its hillock site there are glimpses of deep wood corners, green curtains of pasture rising to rolling moor-sides; amidst old stone, the call of lapwing and lark rise high over the heather-tops.

Climb over the wall onto Fox Lane and turn right down towards Cordwell. Notice a ruined farmhouse below the lane on the left as you pass by tall hollies. On the right and hidden by a yew and entangling undergrowth is Croft's Farm. Both those places have gone the way that

Bank Green is going; to think that in the 1930s more than twenty people lived happily in these three farms!

From this stretch of Fox Lane you will be able to pick out Horsleygate Hall to the north. A large square-built house with fine sash windows and large stables. This is the next hall to be passed. Look for a stile behind the last of the hollies on the left and drop steeply to cross Millthorpe

The Ancient Arch at Horsleygate Old Hall

Brook by a footbridge; go through a gate on the bridle path and immediately follow the wall up on the left to a stile which brings you onto the Owler Bar Road at a corner (map reference: 306/767). Walk 250 yards (225 metres) up the road to the left and turn right (the signpost says 'Holmesfield') to the bush-banked gates of Horsleygate Hall.

Though old this is more recent than Horsleygate Old Hall further up the lane and the front portion of the house has been added within the last two centuries. This was the home of the Wilsons for most of the twentieth century, owners of many of the acres you have crossed and many of the old buildings seen. This is the fourth Holmesfield Hall and now you face a climb of 310 feet (95 metres) to Lidgate on the hilltop to the north. Finding the footpath is not easy here. Walk along past the Hall and where the rhododendrons end search behind the verge-side shrubs on the left for the stepping-stones over the wall.

The first few minutes are occupied by walking up beside the high garden wall, in tree cover. Then continue up across a large pasture field with a sprinkling of gorse bushes to an outlying barn and stable.

Go over the stile in the wall ahead and up the steep field-edge with wonderful views to the south-east, of Barlow Vale, and west, of the more dramatic steeps of Smeekley, the moors behind and nearer Cockshutts Wood. This large field is the Great Sheppah, having an area of 10½ acres (4.5 hectares), and is best seen from the edge of the Meek fields by Moorhall.

You soon reach the Holmesfield–Owler Bar road at the Robin Hood Inn at **Lidgate**.

Fanshawe Gate Lane faces you so cross the main road and walk along the lane for nearly ½ mile (0.75 km) to the old hamlet of Fanshawe Gate. At the foot of the steepest gradient Fanshawe Gate Old Hall stands back on the left, its drive guarded by fine, ball-topped gateposts. The old dovecote at the garden wall is in a good state of repair and the only one you will see on this circular walk. The Fanshawe family lived here for a long period.

Henry Fanshawe was Queen Elizabeth I's first Remembrancer and by his will of 1579 he left charities for the establishment of Dronfield Grammar School. His brother, Thomas, became the second Remembrancer. Quite appropriately John and Cynthia Ramsden are the present owners of Fanshawe Gate – both of them Old Dronfeldians.

The Pigeon Cote, Fanshawe Gate

Pass on down the lane, past Owler Lee, and in less than ½ mile (0.75 km) from Fanshawe Gate the gables of Woodthorpe Hall peer above the trees ahead.

Woodthorpe, literally 'the settlement in the wood', stands at the bottom of Holmesfield Park and looks southwards to the steep ridge on which Holmesfield village itself stands. Behind the Hall the fields drop to the wide north-running valley which contains Totley, Millhouses and Beauchief (now part of Sheffield's suburbs) and is drained by the Totley Brook, the infant which becomes the River Sheaf lower down. On the fields to either side of the Sheaf the town (now a city) grew, famous for its cutlery and named after its position by the river.

The walk back to Holmesfield is made by way of Holmesfield Park Wood, a dense piece of woodland on the northward slope from Holmesfield down towards Totley Brook. According to Tilley, 'the memory of the Deincourts, lords of the manor after the Norman Conquest, is still perpetuated by the plantation, some short distance from the back of the church, being styled "Holmesfield Park". The moat, now all grown over with grass, is still traceable, which surrounded the Castle or homestead of this old and baronial family'. Walk back along the lane from Woodthorpe Hall for 300 yards (274 metres) and on a rightward bend take the track leading off up the wood (map reference: 316/785). Keep to the main path, rising all the time, and in less than ⅔ mile (1 km) a walled lane is joined by a modern bungalow. A couple of minutes' walk brings you to the main road at **Holmesfield**. On the right as you come down the last yards of the lane are the former buildings of

Holmesfield Hall. This is another place with a long and interesting history. To see the house properly you should go right along the main road past the main entrance gate. You will now see the rather low, grey house. In the front garden is an ancient yew and over the front door is the carved stone coat of arms of the Burton family, showing the lambrequin. Above are three helmets, topped by the three crests to which this branch of the Burton family were entitled: 'on a ducal coronet a wyvern; on a natural mount a beacon; on a ducal coronet a cypress tree'.

The Hall was a home of Francis Burton, Lord of Dronfield and Sheriff of the county in 1669, and was owned by the Morgan family for more than two centuries thereafter. William Morgan was listed on the Juries of the Courts Baron on 20th September 1748. Though the ancient wainscoting in the hall has had layers of whitewash coated over it the elaborated Burton ceiling is still well preserved. In recent years the ancient outbuildings have been converted to private houses and the atmosphere of this former single holding has been lost.

On the left as you come down the lane from Holmesfield Park to the main road is the church, mentioned at the beginning of this walk. St Swithin's was re-built in 1826 and commands as fine a view today as then. From its tower on a clear day the towers of Lincoln Cathedral can be seen, and on most days in the year much of the walk we have just completed is visible.

WALK 3

Seven Hathersage Halls

Outline:	**Hathersage, Hazelford, Highlow, Offerton, Shatton, North Lees, Moorseats, Hathersage**
Map:	**OS: 1:25,000 Outdoor Leisure Sheet 1 'The Peak District – Dark Peak Area'**
	OS: 1:25,000 Outdoor Leisure Sheet 24 'The Peak District – White Peak Area'
Distance:	**12 miles/19 km**
Parking:	**Public car park, Oddfellows Road, Hathersage**

Tradition has it that one of the medieval Eyres – that well-known Hope Valley family name – who was probably living at Highlow Hall or North Lees on the wild hills above Hathersage, built a hall for each of his seven sons, each hall being in sight of the others. This would be to offer some measure of protection, to facilitate the passing of messages by signals and with a quaint touch of the romantic. A pleasant walk can be had visiting what are probably six of the seven halls. The walk starts and ends in Hathersage and includes a look at Highlow Hall, most likely the home of Robert Eyre, romantic father of the seven sons.

Route

Proceed from **Hathersage** railway station, under the bridge, along the road towards Grindleford and over the sweep of Leadmill Bridge across the Derwent, by the Plough Inn (left) up to the brow of the hill ahead and make a right turn up the second lane towards Hazelford Hall. Very soon the corner is turned up the steepening lane and the old hall comes into sight. Gables capped by gritstone balls for decoration, ancient leaded lights, and a garden showing loving care are some of the features of the place. The old outbuildings are especially worthy of note, whilst the best views of the hall are obtained by looking back after walking along the lane some distance.

Continue along the lane now until it makes a sharp turn to the left where a track leads on ahead. Turn right here, down a lane towards Hogg Hall but go through a stile in the gate-side ahead instead of turning down to the house. Down one steep pasture field, with Broadhey Farm (ivy-clad) opposite, over a small humpback bridge then turn up right through hawthorn bushes and along the lane to its junction with Abney Lane (map reference: 232/804).

Turn up to the left and in 1 mile (1.5 km) the buildings of **Highlow Hall** come into sight ahead. The old house stands beyond the fine range of outbuildings so you must walk on the lane, noticing the unusual gritstone arch topped with balls guarding the gate to the garden. Walk along the lane a little way so that a backward view can be had. You will see the ancient gazebo standing on the edge of the paddock wall and the large gateposts leading up to the Hall. If tradition is reliable here this must be the oldest of the halls you will visit today, for the father of the

seven sons is reputed to have lived here. And a Robert Eyre was living here in the latter half of the fifteenth century with fourteen children.

Go back along the lane, down past the Hall towards Hathersage, and in a few yards turn sharp left along the ancient trackway signposted 'Callow Farm'. The lane dips down to cross Dunge Clough and on up the hill. At the fork to Callow Farm keep up left and in a short distance the angle eases. Look on the left for the stone pillar called Robin Hood's Stoop. Here tradition again tells that the famous outlaw shot an arrow from this point into the churchyard at Hathersage – almost 1½ miles (2.4 km) distant, as the arrow flies.

The prospect is wide from here. Four of the halls can be seen: Crookhill by its plantation above Ashopton 4½ miles (7.25 km) away and the only hall of the seven that you will not visit today, North Lees towards the head of Hood Brook under Stanage Edge (map reference: 235/835),

Moorseats in the trees above Hathersage church, and Highlow nearby to the right.

A fifth hall is almost visible, for **Offerton** is less than ½ mile (0.75 km) along the lane beyond Robin Hood's Stoop and very soon the well-proportioned house comes into sight, down the slope below the lane. Time will be well spent looking more closely at Offerton. Pass the stile on the left where the lane drops down steeply by ancient beeches reminiscent of Unthank. Look at the rear of the Hall from the upper gate then go down by Offerton House (on the left). Go below and look at the graceful archway leading into the Hall and farmyard, then climb back up the hill to the stile at the corner.

Climb the stile and walk along the moorland way towards Shatton. Soon a wall runs alongside the track on the right-hand. Presently this swings away down the slope towards Banktop Barn but you proceed along and steadily uphill, joining the old lane coming over the moors from Abney and Brough down to Shatton village. This lane is reached over 1 mile (1.5 km) west of Offerton at a gateway with a gatepost bearing a bench mark – 1000 feet (305 metres) above sea level (map reference: 201/815). Turn right down the steep lane, entering **Shatton** village in ¾ mile (1.25 km).

Offerton Hall from the south-east

In the centre of the old village of gritstone built farms and cottages turn left, along the footpath overlooking the ford across the stream draining Shatton Moor and along the ancient sunken lane (suggesting concealment from enemies or an old boundary in years gone by). In ¾ mile (1.25 km) you will see the old manor house of Shatton Hall, down across a field on the left. The Eyres were probably living at Shatton Hall 400 years ago. The Tudor windows of the large living-rooms have leaded lights, odd ones which open with the aid of the original catches.

Go back now, down the lane to Shatton and past the ford. Here, on the left, is Wheat Hay Farm which is of great age. At the centre of the village again turn left down the lane, passing the ivy-covered Homestead at Nether Shatton, fifth of the seven halls you are viewing today. This place was once used for the sorting and counting of sheep, evidence of which can still be seen in the low wall in front of the farm. A tiny window at the joining of house and outbuildings illuminates a room once used as a cheese store, while down the lane a few yards the ancient barns formerly belonging to this place are seen on the left converted to dwellings.

Quarter of a mile (0.5 km) down the lane the River Noe is crossed at Shatton Bridge just above its confluence with the River Derwent. Immediately after crossing the bridge turn right along the main road from Hathersage to Hope. Turn left in a few yards (straight after crossing the bridge over the Derwent) along the road passing **Bamford** Railway Station, and a few yards beyond the railway station turn right up Saltergate Lane. Walk up the lane for nearly ½ mile (1 km) and at the top, where a private road comes in, turn right over a stile in the hedgerow and make your way across and steadily down the slope of the golf course. Drop into a wooded valley ahead and cross the stream draining from Bamford Moor by a new footbridge for golfers (map reference: 214/827) up the other side by a well-made path and across the second part of the course, passing close by an old barn. Just beyond the barn cross the boundary fence and into a pasture field.

Follow the path across and down to the brook. Now up through four fields and three more 'squeezer' stiles to Thorp Farm. Up the lane a short way you meet the by-road coming up from Hathersage towards the open moors. Turn left along the lane and then right in a few yards, at a fork, past Birley Farm and down the hill through a wonderful wood where fungi stand in mixed profusion every autumn. Soon the gables and chimney stacks below on the right herald Brookfield Manor. This is the back of the big house with a misty past. Part of the present fabric bears the date 1646 but little seems to be known of the fine house standing at the end of a drive from Hathersage, through its own tree-studded park by Hood Brook.

Over the little Brookfield Bridge you carry on up the lane behind the Manor for 100 yards (80 metres), passing a modern house (Bronte Cottage) on the left.

A stony track leads up through a gate in the left-hand wall to North Lees Hall, the gables of which can be seen from the lane. This is the sixth of the seven halls, perhaps the most fascinating architecturally. It's a steep pull up the track but eventually the great tower at the end of the Hall peers over the garden wall. Now thought to be designed by the great Robert Smythson, architect of Hardwick and Woollaton, the date 1594 appears in plaster moulding within. The Vesseys lived here in the eighteenth century but in Victorian times the Eyres returned to their Hope Valley roots.

Going up the stony lane beyond the house you get a further glimpse of ancient beauty. The whole steading is cloaked to west and north by finely matured trees, tall standing and 'atmosphere-producing' on windy days and winter days. Up behind the house is the long range of farm buildings – signs here of alteration, for a number of the loose-box doors are sealed with stone to half their height to make windows. Here is another example of a very old cruck building. North Lees Hall is now used by the Vivat Trust and let out for holidays; the farm is Broomfield College's hill farm unit.

Down the drive the way you came, turn right to pass Bronte Cottage then turn left immediately before crossing the Hood Brook. The path crosses close behind Brookfield Manor and on through fields, following the farm track.

A path branches off (left) directly towards the spire of Hathersage Parish church. At the foot of the last, steep rise to the church turn left, through a rough pasture and look for a mysterious stone gateway on the left. Through the door here and start the long pull up to Moorseats.

Moorseats always spells romantic seclusion to me, after the walk up from the valley-bottom bustle. The hall may have been completed by the thirteenth century but there have been additions – in the seventeenth and nineteenth centuries. Suggestions of sanctuary for some Jesuit priest during the persecutions are found in the windows in the south wall, which have no coincidence with present floors. Moorseats is a Bronte relic. Charlotte knew it well when staying at Hathersage vicarage in 1845 and modelled it as the home of the Rivers family in her 'Jane Eyre'. Moorseats stands a mile and three-quarters (2.75 km) north-east of Highlow and is easily visible from the vicinity of the latter hall; it stands about three-quarters of a mile (1.25 km) south-south-east of North Lees. This suggests to me that North Lees had definite associations with the other two halls, at least, for it does stand to the north of them. Moorseats has fine yews, and a ghost which walks the garden beneath their branches.

To reach **Hathersage** and the end of the walk take the lane that curves round to the east, to Carrhead Farm (map reference: 240/822). Go by the farm and down the track towards the valley and enter the sunken lane that leads in 400 yards (350 metres) down to the first habitations of the village, near the church, where yews shade the traditional tomb of Little John and the clock chimes out through the tall trees to the old hillside halls.

WALK 4

Edale to the Higher Shelf Stones and Return

Outline:	**Edale, Grinds Brook, Crowden Head, the Northern Edge, Ashop Clough, Featherbed Moss, Higher Shelf Stones, Lady Clough, Blackden Moor, Grinds Brook, Edale**
Map:	**OS: 1:25,000 Outdoor Leisure Sheet 1 'The Peak District – Dark Peak Area'**
Distance:	**15¼ miles/24.5 km**
Parking:	**Edale car park**

Though Edale is such a mecca for ramblers the Woodlands Valley beyond Kinder Scout is actually more centrally situated for the true 'bog trotter' with the wilds of Bleaklow to the north and Kinder Scout to the south and west. However, it is not a very long excursion to cross Kinder Scout from Edale and wander onto the nearer eminences of the Bleaklow massif, notably the Higher Shelf Stones.

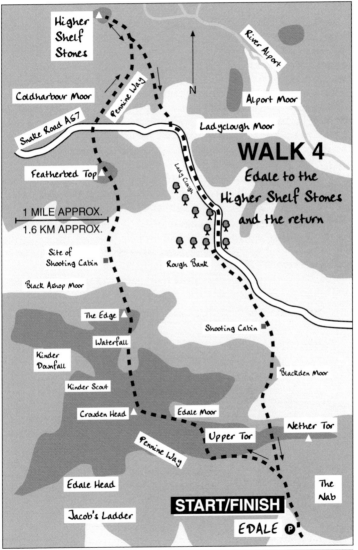

Higher Shelf Stones

Coldharbour Moor

Pennine Way

Snake Road A57

Featherbed Top

1 MILE APPROX.
1.6 KM APPROX.

Site of Shooting Cabin

Black Ashop Moor

The Edge

Waterfall

Kinder Downfall

Kinder Scout

Crowden Head

Pennine Way

Edale Head

Jacob's Ladder

River Alport

Alport Moor

Ladyclough Moor

WALK 4
Edale to the Higher Shelf Stones and the return

Lady Clough

Rough Bank

Shooting Cabin

Blackden Moor

Edale Moor

Upper Tor

Nether Tor

The Nab

START/FINISH

EDALE P

N

Route

Walk northwards through **Edale** village, to the road-head, and cross the bridge over the Grinds Brook which used to mark the southern end of the 250 mile long Pennine Way. Up through the trees on the far side of the brook is Grindslow House. A large, well-proportioned house, this was the home of the Misses Champion, hostesses to ramblers in the days when Kinder Scout was strictly guarded grouse moor. Pasture fields, a mixed copse, the crossing of Golden Clough Brook, and you are out in the wild hollow drained by the well-known, well-loved Grinds Brook. As you ascend by the wide, brown track the valley sides close in. Up on the left is the top of Grindslow Knoll (1900 feet/580 metres), a beautifully-proportioned hill when seen from Nether or Upper Tors, high up on your right as you ascend to the source of the brook. In a little over 1½ miles (2.4 km) from Edale the main stream turns to the north (right), and you follow this up a series of gritstone steps right onto the plateau.

Up on the summit plateau an unusual terrain is revealed: rolling contours, bilberry, crowberry and acid-loving grasses (e.g. molinia). The whole summit tableland is capped with deep peat, chocolate and acid. This cap is eroded by steep-sided groughs (drainage trenches), some narrow enough to jump, others six or more yards wide, some a foot deep and others ten feet deep. Route finding is difficult for the stranger, even

Grindslow House, Edale and Upper Tor

in clear weather, and in mist or at night the expert and regular walker's route-finding can be tested to the full.

As you climb out of the top of the gorge of upper Grinds Brook two upright gritstone blocks forming a 'split-tor' will be noticed 30 yards (27 metres) to the west. If you stand on or by this and look north-west the ridge of higher peatland will be seen on a clear day; make for this and a cairn will be found at **Crowden Head** (2070 feet/630 metres). This is at the heart of the Kinder Scout massif and from it drains the River Kinder to the Goyt, Mersey and Irish Sea, and the Noe, Crowden, Grinds, Blackden, and Fair Brooks to the Derwent, Trent and North Sea.

If lucky the northward view on a clear day, especially in winter anti-cyclonic conditions, will reveal the ridge of Bleaklow and beyond, 10½ miles (16.5 km) away, Home Moss, topped by its television transmission mast. If the mast is visible make for it, keeping slightly left (west) of it so as to avoid the steep drop into the clough occupied by Fair Brook.

A mile (1.5 km) north of Crowden Head stands the fine upper valley of the Fairbrook with a grand view down into the upper Woodlands Valley, thickly carpeted by Forestry Commission coniferous plantations, part of Hope Forest. Keep to the plateau top, west of the clough, and make due north for the 2049 foot (624 metre) spot-height on **The Edge** (map reference: 093/898). This is Kinder Scout's bold northern escarp-ment, cliffy in parts and looking out over Black Ashop Moor, the defile of Ashop Clough (running parallel with The Edge), Featherbed Moss and the far outlines of Bleaklow.

Try to pick out Upper Gate Clough from the top of The Edge, running up on the opposite side of Ashop Clough, and make straight for this. If visibility is poor steer north-north-west from this 2049 foot (624 metre) spot-height, reaching Ashop Clough after a steady ¾ mile (1.2 km) descent. In either event you should come down to the River Ashop near the site of the old **shooting cabin** on the far bank. There is a plank bridge here to cross the river. Here is the east–west Snake Path from Hayfield to the Snake Inn. Cross this and ascend the steep banks north, keeping Upper Gate Clough on the immediate right. You will notice that the vegetation pattern has changed: the River Ashop seems to be a natural boundary between the bilberry, heather and crowberries of Kinder Scout and the acid, often wet, boggy grassland of Bleaklow.

For 1½ miles (2.4 km) make for the north, over the smooth, 1785 foot (544 metre) top of **Featherbed Top** and slightly down to the summit of the Snake Pass (A57 Sheffield–Glossop road). Now bear north-north-east, across the paved section of Doctor's Gate on **Coldharbour Moor** (see Walk 9). In a little more than ½ mile (0.75 km) from the road Crooked Clough will be overlooked on the left, descending towards Glossop as Shelf Brook. Why Crooked Clough, I don't know; there are many cloughs topographically more serpentine!

When a small waterfall is reached (at approximately map reference: 095/945) in the now-shallow clough, cross to the west (left) side and make for the obvious eminence slightly north of west, the **Higher Shelf Stones**. What a feeling of a 'real' summit the last few minutes' climb gives you! With the rise from the wide, smooth shoulders around, it is ascent into free air, with views all round. Only two other tops in the Peak National Park carry the same 'summit sense' for me: Grindslow Knoll and Shutlingsloe. This hill's name would seem to be derived from the fact that it overlooks Shelf Brook, doubtless so-named due to the exposed gritstone strata forming its stepped or shelved bed – Shelf Moor, Shelf Moss and Shelf Benches seem to originate in the same way.

In bad weather you will know you are on the top as there is a trig point here. On an unusually clear January day I had the good luck to see not only the high, white smoke clouds above Stocksbridge and Hope, but also the district around Burnley and, beyond Oldham, towards the Lancashire coast. On that breezeless day of shining sun there was a quilt of compacted snow patches left on Bleaklow's ruddy slopes – some of the smaller patches turned out to be mountain hares.

Less than 100 yards (80 metres) to the north-east of the 2039 foot (621 metre) summit are the remains of a US Air Force Super Fortress which crashed so near the summit during the Berlin Air Lift. The torn and twisted remains add a certain morbid romance to this section of Bleaklow and an interesting half an hour can be spent looking at dented pistons, polished pipes and undercarriage mechanisms.

You are 8¼ miles (13.25 km) from Edale and the return is by a different route, more varied than the outward journey. Make for the south-east, aiming to reach the Snake Road where Upper North Grain joins the main Lady Clough (map reference: 101/929). There are many 'grains' in the Bleaklow massif and the name is derived from the Old Norse word grein, a fork of a river or, in dialect, a small valley branching

View to Blackden Clough and Fairbrook Naze across Hope Woodlands Valley

from another. Hence this particular hollow is the uppermost of the north-ward-leading valleys (or cloughs) off the main valley. A mile and three-quarters (2.75 km) south-east of the Higher Shelf Stones the road will be reached.

Follow the road down towards the Snake Inn for about 2 miles (3.25 km) and turn off right (west) where the Hayfield track – the Snake Path – goes down through Hope Forest. At the River Ashop turn south and follow one bank or the other until the confluence of the Fairbrook with the Ashop. Notice the bold brow of Fairbrook Naze far up the clough to the west as you cross the Fair Brook. On the far side of the confluence an ascending path will be seen to the south, rising steeply up the shoulder of Wood Moor and then out of sight. Follow this; it is reminiscent of an alpine path to a high hut. The cabin that used to stand on Wood Moor was vandalised and later completely removed – a sad loss for responsible ramblers in bad weather.

Wood Moor cabin stood on the 1250 foot (381 metre) contour and to reach the Edale Valley still entails 3 miles (4.75 km) of walking and

650 feet (198 metres) of ascent onto the lowest part of Edale Moor. From Wood Moor make due south, avoiding the skyline of Seal Edge to the left and contouring round and slightly up the slopes overlooking upper Blackden Brook. After crossing the headwaters of the brook continue south, at about 170 degrees. Once on the highest part of this area of Edale Moor the Edale Valley quickly comes into view and the edge of the plateau between Upper and Nether Edges is reached (map reference: 117/877).

I have descended the 800 feet (244 metres) from the plateau edge to the track in the bottom of Grinds Brook in 2½ minutes, in failing light and with a scattering of wet snow, so even are the contours; and only on the lower boulder-strewn bracken slopes is special care needed.

Once in Lower Grinds Brook it is less than 1 mile (1.5 km) to **Edale**, through the copse, over the fields and across the bridge.

WALK 5

The Westend and Uppermost Derwent Valleys

Outline:	**Westend Mouth, Westend Valley, Grinah Grain and Stones, Derwent Head, Swains Greave, the uppermost Derwent, Slippery Stones, Westend Mouth (or Derwent Head, Deep Grain, Alport Dale, Fagney Clough, Westend Mouth)**
Map:	**OS 1:25,000 Outdoor Leisure Sheet 1 'The Peak District – Dark Peak Area'**
Distance:	**10½ miles/16.5 km**
Parking:	**Mouth of River Westend (Map ref: 155/928)**

For the true hill-walker Bleaklow and its surrounding outliers is probably the best place in the Peak Park with regard to remoteness and the wide-open vista. There is nowhere else quite like this; it is Britain's only true desert, both vegetationally and topographically, and is barely less than Kinder Scout in elevation.

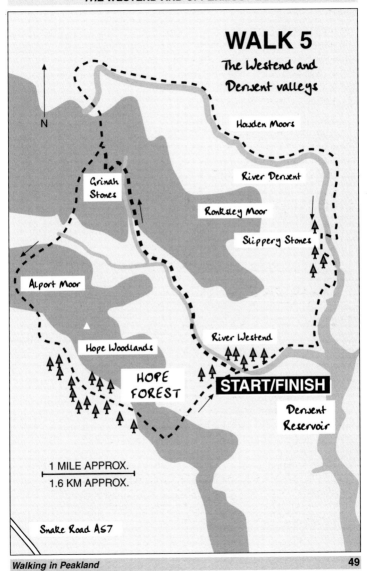

WALK 5

The Westend and
Derwent valleys

N

Howden Moors

Grinah Stones

River Derwent

Ronksley Moor

Slippery Stones

Alport Moor

Hope Woodlands

River Westend

HOPE FOREST

START/FINISH

Derwent Reservoir

1 MILE APPROX.

1.6 KM APPROX.

Snake Road A57

Route

This walk is the first of three in this guide in the eastern sector of Bleaklow. More than 6 miles (9.5 km) above the turn-off to Derwent from the Sheffield–Glossop road there is a large inlet on the western shore of Howden reservoir; this is the **Westend** inlet. At its farthest reach the River Westend meanders in, rich and peaty from its moorland wandering on the shoulders above.

Leave the road here (map reference: 155/928) and follow the track through the larch and spruce plantation, ignoring the path leading directly up the slope on the left with a signpost indicating 'Open Country' and a route to the Alport Valley. In a quarter of an hour from the road the plantation ends and a rough bridge takes you over the river. Ahead is the open valley of the Westend, green on a sunny day and spattered with the scattered remains of the ancient oak, hawthorn and rowan forest at 1200 feet (365 metres) above sea level. A long way away and at the head of the valley the dim crest of the Grinah Stones is visible, like an impregnable fortress on the distant moor-top.

You follow up the right (true left) bank of the stream and in another quarter of an hour go through a gap in a wall ahead. In a moment you will see an ancient copse of alders ahead, sheltered in a curve of the valley. High above on the right is a scar where the shales of Ridgewalk Moor have slipped.

Up through the old alders, the track slowly turns up to the right and onto a spur of the moor at 1300 feet (396 metres), above the confluence of the Grinah Grain and the young Westend.

Keep along to the north now, high above the Grinah Grain's right (true left) bank. Across the Grain, at about the same level as the path, the outlet from the water-table hereabouts can be detected. Below it is the descent line of water, and luscious plants and sponge moss, leading directly down to the stream. Ten minutes more along the side of this tributary valley notice a delectable spot below – a silver birch overhangs the slabby bed of the stream where water cascades. In summer the whole bank behind is a patchwork of various greens, of bilberry and tussock grass and infant bracken poking up (map reference: 135/954).

Five minutes beyond this viewpoint the path drops to the water and a crossing is made to the other side. Now follow the stream up its bank, slowly climbing to the crest of Ridgewalk Moor not far from the Grinah

*The Bleaklow
Summit Ridge
from Grinah
Stones*

Stones. On most days the Stones will be in view over the crest and a comparatively short walk diagonally right through a line of shooting butts and over the heather will bring you to the Sow and Piglet Rocks (reminiscent of Ilkley's Cow and Calf Rocks) at the foot of the great stony ridge dropping from the Stones' top.

Close above to the north are the **Grinah Stones** – forming Bleaklow's boldest brow, cutting out over the southern and central wastes of this highland. Climb the tumbled gritstone blocks to the 1900 foot (579 metre) crest and on this proud brink search the world around for familiar landmarks, foregrounds on other walks. This point can be reached in about 1¾ hours from the road.

On P.P. Burdett's 1767 map of Derbyshire this headland was marked 'Grinah Stone' and earlier, in 1627, it was called 'Graine well Stones'. It is obvious from this reference that Grinah is derived from the old Norse word grein.

Walk north now to gain the watershed of Bleaklow's summit ridge, which runs east–west. Even in misty conditions it is comparatively easy to tell when this ridge has been gained by the change of character of the surface. The going is now over exposed peat with gritstone fragments and powder in the grough-bottoms, and on a clear day the northern moors of Holme Moss become visible ahead. On a grey or hazy day it is interesting to try to pick out the television mast on top of Holme Moss, over 5 miles (8 km) away to the north-west. In certain lights the mast appears and disappears, comes and goes fascinatingly.

Just here, at a little under the 2000 foot (606 metre) contour, is the source of the Derwent – Derbyshire's (and all Peakland's) biggest and best-known river, though comparatively few know this spot. A careful search ½ mile (0.75 km) north-west of the Grinah Stones (map reference: 125/968) will reveal a small oasis upon this desert-top. In summer the water dries up but the marsh grasses remain; in winter the pool fills and is more easily identified. A mile (1.5 km) to the west-south-west are the conspicuous Bleaklow Stones, with Bleaklow Head (another 1½ miles/ 2.5 km farther west) the highest points of the massif, at 2060 feet (633 metres) above sea level.

From the source of the Derwent you can continue down this growing river and so back in a clockwise direction to the River Westend's mouth, **or** turn south and so down Alport Dale and back in an anti-clockwise direction. Let us first briefly consider the latter route.

Turn down the south-facing flank of the main ridge and walk slightly west of south for about 1 mile (1.5 km) down Deep Grain, a tributary clough of the Westend. On reaching the Westend, flowing from right to left as you approach, go straight across and up the moor for another ½ mile (0.75 km) to a shallow 'pass', from where the deep clough containing the River Alport is seen below. Follow the river down for nearly 2½ miles (4 km) until a rectangular coniferous plantation is seen stretching high up the slope above the left bank.

Cross the river and ascend behind (above) this plantation. At the farthest corner (i.e. the south-east corner on the map) turn still further up the slope and out onto **Alport Moor**. Continue south-east along the ridge until a footpath is met striking off to the north-east. Follow this and very soon descend into the mixed woodland above Westend Mouth.

Now to describe the other route back. From the source-pool of the Derwent it is a straightforward task to follow the infant river north down the slope to Swains Greave, reached in ½ mile (0.75 km). This is a smooth-contoured heather basin behind the Barrow Stones. In 1627 the place was called 'Swaines graue head'. Swaine would seem to be of thirteenth-century Scandinavian origin, while Greave comes from the

Old English grafa (a copse or grove, which stood here 600 years ago), and the Old English heafod would have become 'head', or source, of the river by the seventeenth century.

Here the growing stream has cut down through the peat and reached the shales and stones of a former river-bed level. If you stand by the water's edge here you can pick out not only the layers of shales and the peat rising up to 12 feet (3.5 metres) above the present river level, but the remains of the long-vanished woodland can be seen, too.

Whole trunks and branches of silver birch, still with the bark in place, can be pulled from the peat banks, remnants of Swains Greave, or Swaines graue head, of three centuries ago. The probable reason for the 'death' of this wood was the advance of peat beneath the trees' roots, leading to starvation and an accumulation of weak acids. The same state of affairs exists on Hoo Moor, to the west of the lower Goyt Valley, where the trees (many coniferous) are dying for the same reason – a Swains Greave delayed five or six centuries!

Following the **Derwent** down, a gorge-like section is reached in another quarter of an hour. The path follows the left bank. The route is now straightforward again; you simply follow the river on its left bank. All that moor to the left (east) of the Derwent and up as far as the watershed is National Trust property, and for many miles south as far as Dovestone Tor and the Salt Cellar on Derwent Edge.

In less than half an hour beyond the short, gorge-like section you can follow the river close to its bank (a rather time-consuming but interesting way) or cut up on a path on the left, over a shoulder to a line of substantial shooting butts. Below the lowest butt is a newly-made track which can be followed right down the valley past craggy Deer Holes and Mosley Bank to **Slippery Stones**.

Slippery Stones (map reference: 169/951) is nearly 6 miles (9.5 km) below the source of the Derwent, where the ancient Cut Gate trackway from Langsett and Penistone forded the river by slabby, 'slippery' stones *en route* to the Woodlands Valley by way of Rowlee. The old packhorse bridge over the river at Derwent village further downstream was dismantled before Ladybower Reservoir's upper waters had opportunity to submerge it. The stones were numbered and stored in a nearby barn for many years until the bridge was re-erected here at Slippery Stones in 1959 to act as a footbridge for walkers, shepherds and shooters, and as a memorial to that notable rambler and countryman, John Derry, who died in 1937.

Cross the river here and follow the track down through the coniferous plantation, reaching the road-head at Ronksley in a quarter of an hour. The walk is finished by following the road down the side of Howden Reservoir for a 1½ miles (2.5 km) to **Westend** Mouth.

WALK 6

Margery Hill and the Howden Moors

Outline:	**Ronksley, Slippery Stones, Margery Hill, Outer Edge, Howden Edge, Swains Head, Down the Derwent, Slippery Stones, Ronksley**
Map:	**OS 1:25,000 Outdoor Leisure Sheet 1 'The Peak District – Dark Peak Area'**
Distance:	**11½ miles (18.5 km)**
Parking/access:	**Fairholmes, Derwent Dale, then bus service to King's Tree (weekends and bank holidays) or King's Tree, Derwent road-head**

Route

At the end of the road up the west side of the Derwent and Howden reservoirs you can see the site of Ronksley Farm, just across the stepping stones over Linch Clough stream (map reference: 168/940). This is, in fact, Ronksley.

The construction of the Howden and Derwent reservoirs between 1900 and 1912 led to the development of 'Tin Town', a settlement of huts and shacks housing 400 labourers and their families on the western side of Derwent Dale at Birchinlee. By the beginning of World War I the 'town' had been torn down and so had thirteen lovely old farms, flooded or made derelict by the new 'lakes'. There was Westend Farm, Ridge Farm and Abbey Farm, and many others left to ruin. There was Marebottom, still standing below Howden's great impounding wall, and

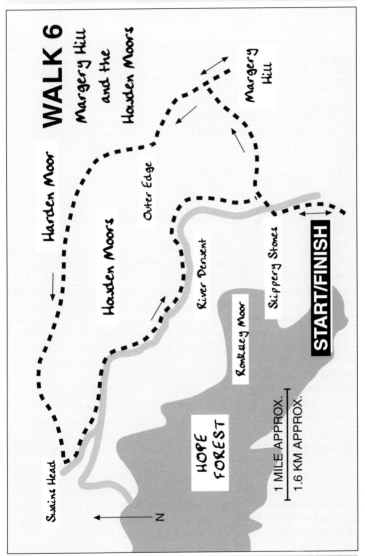

WALK 6

Margery Hill
and the
Howden Moors

Harden Moor

Margery Hill

Outer Edge

Howden Moors

River Derwent

Swains Head

Ronksley Moor

Slippery Stones

START/FINISH

HOPE
FOREST

1 MILE APPROX.
1.6 KM APPROX.

N

Howden Farm – not to mention ancient Ronksley at the Linch Clough crossing.

Most of these farms were standing in the Middle Ages and had monastic connections. Abbey Grange was a property of the monks of Welbeck. Derwent Hall was built in 1672 by the Balguys, a Derbyshire family traceable back to the thirteenth century. Most of these buildings have gone beneath the water, maintained in memory by the aged and by field and moor names and old boundaries.

Walk north through the coniferous plantation to **Slippery Stones**, reached in quarter of an hour from Ronksley. Cross the re-erected pack-horse bridge over the Derwent. It was built in medieval times and in 1682 was in great need of repair, being the worst of the county's nine bridges needing such treatment. The estimated cost of repairs in that year was £100. As mentioned in Walk 5, this bridge was removed from its site in Derwent village before the Ladybower Reservoir flooded that area of the dale.

Follow the footpath to the left (north) for 200 yards (180 metres) and cross Cranberry Clough stream as it comes down from the eastward moor. Turn up this clough and follow the ancient trackway up the steep slopes between Bull Clough (left) and Cranberry Clough (right). You must ascend almost 800 feet (243 metres) from Slippery Stones to the wild, wide pass on the skyline. A backward glance as you climb reveals more and more of the upper Derwent and its eroded features – a deep, river-worn trench cut into the High Peak plateau. Across the river and extending up the far slopes are the old, neglected fields of Mosley Bank and Ox Hey, with the Westend, Alport and Ashop trenches receding into the western haze, while Kinder Scout frowns greyly beyond.

In 1¼ miles (2 km) from Slippery Stones the top of the ancient Cut Gate track is reached, at 1724 feet (425 metres) above sea level. This track was mentioned as 'Cartgate' in a 1571 document, and until 1900 the employees of a local farmer and of the Duke of Norfolk repaired it annually for horse traffic, so that the farmers of Derwent Woodlands could ride to Penistone market. In bad weather and at night it is very easy to lose the track on the top of the moor and without a compass and map the stranger could spend a long and tiring time finding a route down to a valley. On the loveliest summer day these high wastes of peat and acid grasses, of boulders and bilberry are still wild.

From Slippery Stones to the top of Cut Gate the route has been over National Trust property and now you turn south along the boundary for ⅓ mile (0.5 km) to the summit of **Margery Hill** (1793 feet/546 metres). The old name was Margery Pyke or Nabb and the trig point topped summit marks the highest boundary point between the old Wigtwizzle Common (to the east) and Howden pasture-lands.

Just below Margery Hill, to the west, is Wilfrey Edge, dropping Derwentwards. On this edge is a curious stone with a hole in it called 'Wilfred's Needle' (after the peep-hole in Saint Wilfred's cell in Ripon Cathedral crypt). According to the great Peakland authority G.H.B Ward, the boys of Howden and Wigtwizzle had the habit of creeping through the hole while the 'commoner-shepherds regularly gathered and marked the boundaries of the respective out-pastures'. A century ago the local inhabitants knew 'Wilfrey Nield' and 'Wilfey Edge' but today they are almost forgotten place-names.

From Margery Hill top turn back towards the north and cross Cut Gate, continuing for 1½ miles (2.5 km) to the north-west. A last heather-rise not far from the line of stakes marking the Wigtwizzle Common–Howden boundary leads to the top of **Outer Edge** with its little cliff on the western side. All around the summit on an early summer day can be found blinking clusters of cloudberry (Rubus chamaemorous) in full bloom. The ground is lit by a sea of white, purest white; and though the fresh green leaves of this lonely plant facing the sky are always a thrill to find, their loveliness is doubled at this season of flower by the dazzling, dancing petals.

Continue now over the almost featureless moor-top between the headwaters of tributaries draining to the Derwent on the left and the Porter or Little Don on the right. The 4 mile (6.4 km) walk from Margery Hill to Swains Head (1679 feet/570 metres) is not easy in poor visibility for the contours are widely spaced and there are few landmarks. Follow the National Trust boundary on Howden Edge and Featherbed Moss – with the conspicuous Horse Stone on the 1727 foot (527 metre) knoll to the south often visible – to the Yorkshire–Derbyshire county boundary at **Swains Head** (map reference: 133/983).

Here you can see, on clear days, the television mast on Holme Moss nearly 5 miles (8 km) distant on the north-western horizon. You can also see the head of the Derwent above Swains Greave a mile away to the south-south-west (see Walk 5).

Turn south, following the vague trench-line marked here and there with stakes, and soon the little Derwent is reached, flowing from right to left. If time allows you may wish to turn upstream into that remotest Peakland hollow and listen to the silence. Otherwise turn left and follow the Derwent down the 5 miles (8 km) by the big Deer Holes landslip and **Slippery Stones** to Ronksley, as described in Walk 5.

The round is nearly 12 miles (18.5 km) and can be done quite comfortably in 4½ or 5 hours, though it is pleasanter to take most of the day and thereby enjoy the solitude and wide-angled views to all skies and the occasional sounds and calls of the moor.

In Alport Dale

Gritstone beds, oil shales, Alport Castles,
Grains in the Water, clough names, waterfalls,
Alport Head, an adventurous inventor, forestry
plantations, the Alport Lovefeast

Alport Dale is truly 'the jewel of Bleaklow' of an earlier chronicler. This deep green trench runs for 5½ miles (9 km) north from Alport Bridge – where the Alport joins the Ashop (map reference: 142/896) – up to the summit of Bleaklow Hill.

The river rises on the wild, acid-peat moors overlying carboniferous millstone grit and down its entire course to the confluence with the Ashop it cascades over typical gritstone 'shelves' indicative of the level stratification of this rock series hereabouts. Millstone grit is a group of mud-stones and shales with beds of grit and sandstone. At Alport the Rough Rock group is exposed and the tops of the moorland above consist of shale grit. Some of the shales inter-bedded with the grit and sandstone in the dale are oil-bearing, though not sufficiently richly to be exploitable economically. Some of this oil shale can be seen in the high banks just above Alport Bridge.

High up on the eastern slope of Alport Dale 1 mile (1.5 km) above Alport Bridge is Britain's biggest landslip, Alport Castles. Millions of tons of shales and grit have slipped down the slopes towards the river and left unstable cliffs and tumbled heaps of boulders and debris, overshadowed by the Tower. This is the most conspicuous feature of Alport Castles, a great tower-like mass that has left the 'parent' slopes but has not toppled far. The top of the Tower is 1450 feet (442 metres) above sea level – a little lower than the top of the big cliff. This whole topsy-turvy world is relatively little known but well worth investigating. Every time I go there a new feature is revealed: a ring ouzel's nest or a hidden pool or a new overhang. From the summit of the Tower or from the cliff behind a wonderful vista opens out on a clear day.

Four and a half miles (7.2 km) upstream from Alport Bridge is fascinating Grains in the Water. Here the valley suddenly opens out into the more airy world of Bleaklow in the region of the Swamp. You are at 1550 feet (472 metres) above the sea. Hern Clough comes in from the west and joins the little Alport as it turns from its south-running way towards the east. The name Grains in the Water dates back to 1840 and, remembering that 'grain' can mean 'a fork in the river', it obviously refers rather romantically to this forking of the Hern Clough and Alport waters. The Swamp, by the way, was first referred to by this name in 1843.

The business of clough (or valley) names is very interesting. There are scores of named cloughs on Bleaklow, most getting their nomenclature from geographical position. Near Fork Grain, for example, flows into the infant Alport very 'near' to the latter's source on Alport Head – in fact, it is the first stream to enter on the western side below the source. Another is Swint Clough which drains to the Alport by Alport Castles Farm. In the Old English of 1285 it was Swynecloueheved, 'the top of the valley where swine graze'. But there are others to be traced, falling to the Alport from east and west.

There are few waterfalls in Peakland and Alport Dale has three of them. Admittedly they are far from dramatic but are noisy and picturesque. They occur in the upper, immature, gorge-like section of the Dale, the upper two within a hundred yards of each other where a landslip on the western slopes has blocked the valley floor and caused the river to cut through and over the debris. The upper-most is the most noble, especially after a storm over Bleaklow. The lowest fall of the trio is not far above a meander where Nether Reddale Clough comes in. It is overhung with a single rowan and falls into a deep, circular plunge-pool.

Alport Head is right at the heart of the desert sweeps of Bleaklow. In 1627 it was Alperd Heade, the source of our little gritstone river just below the summit ridge of Bleaklow Hill, the central eminence of the Bleaklow watershed and almost 2050 feet (624 metres) above sea level. Bare peat abounds and, between, wind-and frost-shattered gritstone shining in sun and glistening in rain. Great expanses of gritty debris lie where the peat collects the first drops of the Alport.

Over a century ago an adventurous farmer-cum-mechanic had the idea of carrying some of Alport's water through a short tunnel near Hayridge Farm to drive a cotton mill planned near the confluence of the Alport and the Ashop rivers. The two halves of his hand-dug tunnel never met in the middle and the disheartened farmer and his labourers gave the task up after months of toil! The entrance to the Ashop end of the tunnel can still be seen in the bank a few yards above Alport Bridge, on the southern side of the main road.

When more water was needed to fill Derwent Reservoir over half a century ago water was carried from the Alport to the little dam on the Ashop whence water is piped under Rowlee Pasture into the Derwent Valley 2 miles (3.2 km) away. The Alport half of the farmer's original tunnel was used, it is said, for this purpose. That notable Peakland pioneer rambler, Fred Heardman, used to come through the still-dry Water Board tunnel soon after its construction and so shorten an otherwise long walk over Rowelee Pasture *en route* for Edale from Derwent!

The Alport Valley plantations (planted between the wars) occupy a considerable acreage on the western slopes of the lower Dale from Hey Ridge past Swint Clough as far as Ferny Side. There is also a conspicuous rectangular plantation on the eastern slope. Some groan at the planting of 'regimental' forests by the former Forestry Commission but surely the effect here (as so often elsewhere in wild regions) has been to shelter and break up otherwise bare and monotonous slopes. The view up Alport Dale from Crookstone Knoll has been made far more satisfying by the inclusion of dark green shadows on one side.

The hamlet of Alport is tiny and little visited, standing above the lower reaches of the river on the west bank 1 mile (1.5 km) above Alport Bridge. Because of its isolation it was favourably situated for the continuation of nonconformist worship (as at other remote Pennine settlements) when such practice became illegal under laws passed in the early part of Charles II's reign. John Wesley is reported to have preached on various occasions in a barn belonging to Alport Castles Farm, on his way between Yorkshire and Lancashire.

Deriving from the feasts of charity in early Christian times, the Woodlands Lovefeast is still held in the barn already referred to, on the first Sunday of each July. People from a large area come to the service, to the memory of the old feast of charity when the wealthy brought food for the poor. During the service everyone takes cake and a little water as a mark of Methodist fellowship.

WALK 7

Up the Alport and Down Oyster Clough

Outline:	**Alport Bridge, Alport Castles Farm, Upper Alport Dale, Grains in the Water, Alport Head, Grains in the Water, Over Wood Moss, Oyster Clough, Roman Road, Alport Bridge**
Map:	**OS 1:25,000 Outdoor Leisure Sheet 1 'The Peak District – Dark Peak Area'**
Distance:	**12 miles/19 km**
Parking:	**Alport Bridge, beside A57 (Map ref: 142/896)**

Route

From the noticeboard and footpath sign at Alport Bridge (map reference: 142/896) walk up through the copse to the lane which leads in 20 minutes to Alport hamlet. The Lovefeast barn has its back to you as you enter the gate from the lane. Turn down right and through the farmyard and down to Swint Clough stream. Instead of following the signpost 'To Open Country' cross Swint Clough stream and walk up the dale, between wall and river.

Alport Castles is high up on the right, and just across the river on the crumpled bank is Castles Wood, largely of silver birch. In less than 10 minutes, where the wall cuts ahead to an old, disused meander, keep right of the gate in front and shortly climb the step-ladder stile. Across the dale is the rectangular coniferous plantation, mentioned earlier on the walk from Derwent Head to Westend Mouth. On your side of the river the plantation sweeps close to the valley floor. Continue between forest fence and river.

By the time the last of the plantation is left behind Grindlesgrain Tor is in view ahead, a rather broken expanse of loose shales and gritstone.

Below you the valley floor narrows, guarded by silver birch, ash, rowan, holly, goat willow and hawthorn. While at the water's edge tormentil peep and ferns grow lushly in summer. You can now choose to

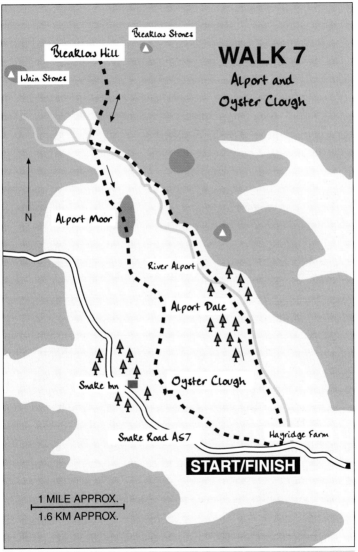

Bleaklow Stones

Bleaklow Hill

Wain Stones

WALK 7
Alport and
Oyster Clough

N

Alport Moor

River Alport

Alport Dale

Oyster Clough

Snake Inn

Snake Road A57

Hayridge Farm

START/FINISH

1 MILE APPROX.
1.6 KM APPROX.

follow the riverside all the way up **Alport Dale** or take a higher path on the opposite slope. If the former is decided upon (a more exciting way up the Alport) an extra hour should be allowed to reach Alport Head. If the latter route is chosen then cut down and across the river and straight up the opposite slope for 150 feet (45 metres), to join a rough path which contours above the river and the difficulties.

Continue along this path and soon the next ½ mile (0.75 km) length of the dale is seen below as a tree-dotted trench. Before the leftward turn at the upper end of this section notice the triple falls below (reminiscent of the Aysgarth Falls on the Ure in miniature).

At the next rightward turn of the river the valley narrows, shadowed by a dripping, mossy outcrop on the far (west) side. Out of sight below, under a single rowan is the lowest of the Alport's celebrated waterfalls (map reference: 117/936). It is not high but certainly picturesque. Being virtually invisible from the path above it is necessary to descend to the rowan to see the water splashing over the shaley step and into the deep, dark pool beneath.

The path loses itself in this vicinity, and so climb straight up the slope until you are about 150 feet (45 metres) above the river level. Here is a better path, and in 200 yards (180 metres) farther north it climbs steeply to suddenly reveal the river meandering ahead between interlocking spurs.

Nearly 2 miles (3.25 km) beyond, the rolling top of Bleaklow can be seen on a clear day. From the path the upper fall, 100 yards (90 metres) above the middle fall, cannot be seen properly so I like to descend again when opposite that middle one and follow the river up to the higher fall, then follow it by its east (true left) bank to Grains in the Water (map reference: 105/947).

If the proper, high path is followed Grains in the Water is reached in less than 1 mile (1.5 km). Here, at 1550 feet (472 metres) above the sea, you turn right to follow the young Alport. Looking up the river from Grains in the Water you can see a rather bold shoulder ½ mile (0.75 km) away and to the left (west) of this is Bleaklow Head (2060 feet/628 metres) topped with gritstone tors, and to the right (east) of the bold brow – and just out of sight – is Bleaklow Hill just above Alport Head, where the river is born just under the sky.

Continue up the infant river, soon reaching the branch of Near Fork Grain, and then the 2000 foot (609 metre) contour is crossed and we

Winter sunset over Lose Hill and Back Tor (Walk 8)

Summit of Back Tor, Derwent Edge (Walk 8)

View north along Stanage Edge from Robin Hood section (Walk 8)

The Hope Valley from Mam Tor, with clouds over Derwent Edge (Walk 10)

Lantern Pike from the Twenty Trees above Hayfield (Walk 11)

Washgates, near Hollinsclough, upper Dove Valley (Three Hills and a River)

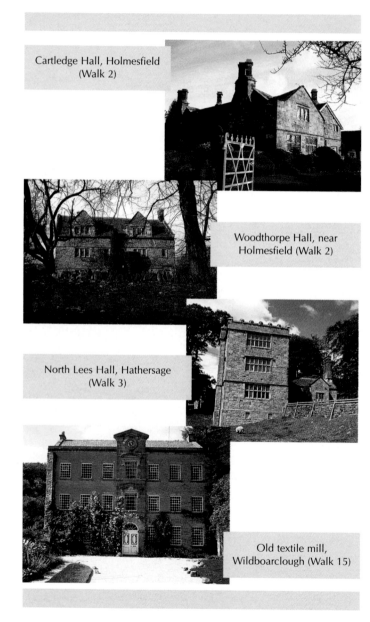

Cartledge Hall, Holmesfield (Walk 2)

Woodthorpe Hall, near Holmesfield (Walk 2)

North Lees Hall, Hathersage (Walk 3)

Old textile mill, Wildboarclough (Walk 15)

stand amid the peaty wastes of grough and bilberry. The grouse call as they rise and desert horizons roll on every hand, grey in cloud and rain, russet on a sunny autumn day and clear green in spring. This is **Bleaklow Hill**, the heart of wildest Peakland where the Alport is born.

Walk down by the river again, as far as Grains in the Water. Now walk towards the south-east for ½ mile (0.75 km) until the watershed is reached. This is known as Over Wood Moss and the skill is now to keep to the very indistinct wastershed (or ridge). In poor visibility a compass is essential – if you are in the deep groughs it is easy to go off course, and if you maintain the swampy course on top it is easy to be diverted hopelessly off course by bog.

After reaching the 1759 foot (536 metre) high Spot Height (map reference: 112/935) turn due south, keeping Nether Reddale Clough on the left. At map reference 112/929 it is possible to look west and on a clear day see the Snake Road nearing its highest point on Featherbed Moss. When the road appears to be going at right-angles to your route turn to the south-east, skirting round the watershed of Nether Reddale Clough (to the left) and above Birchin Clough (right).

In 1 mile (1.5 km) drop down to the head of **Oyster Clough** and see the finely situated shooting cabin at the 'wild end' of the Long Traverse down the clough (map reference: 117/915).

Continue on down the Long Traverse for the ½ mile (0.75 km) of its length, to the mouth of the upper clough, where things open out to reveal Kinder Scout's northern face across the valley – Crookstone Knoll over to the left and Seal Edge ahead. Notice the steep and sweeping track up to Wood Moor. Across Oyster Clough's open mouth is a smaller Alport Castles-type of shaley landslip. This is Cowms Rocks and below it is a ruined stone shooting cabin, while far away down the Woodlands Valley (between Cowms Rocks and Crookstone Knoll from your viewpoint) double-topped Crook Hill is conspicuous, with Bamford Edge and Stanage Edge beyond, over 9 miles (14.5 km) distant.

Drop steeply down to the stream in the clough-bottom where the Roman road crosses above the narrowing of the lower section (hence oyster-like) then continue down the Roman road for 2 miles (3.25 km) to **Hayridge Farm** – described in Walk 9 – and hence along the lane towards Alport hamlet for 200 yards (180 metres) and down the grass and through the trees to Alport Bridge.

WALK 8

The Greater Peakland Circuit

Outline:	**Overstones Farm, Stanage Edge, Derwent Edge, Margery Hill, Howden Moors, Bleaklow, Doctor's Gate, The Edge, Kinder Gates, Kinder Low, Edale Cross, Brown Knoll, Lord's Seat, Mam Tor, Lose Hill, Win Hill, Yorkshire Bridge, Sheepwash Bank, Overstones Farm**
Map:	**OS 1:25,000 Outdoor Leisure Sheet 1 'The Peak District – Dark Peak Area'**
Distance:	**42 miles/67 km (or with additions, 50 miles/ 80 km)**
Parking:	**Car park near Overstones Farm (Map ref: 248/829)**

As far as I know this long walk had been completed twice before I first set out to follow the route. The first time it was accomplished in 17½ hours and on the second occasion in 15½. The heavy rain of weeks had been dried out by days of sun and it was May, with many hours of light. I would suggest that to be enjoyed to the full this walk be under-taken only in the period from April to August unless the route is known or the walker is not worried by walking in the dark. At other times of the year it will prove a race with time and darkness.

Route

Leave the area of Overstones Farm (map reference: 248/829) above Hathersage as early as possible, say 5am. Go in a northerly direction up onto the top of **Stanage Edge** and walk along this fine gritstone edge for 2½ miles (4 km) to Crow Chin, passing High Neb (1502 feet/458 metres) *en route* after 2 miles (3 km).

At Crow Chin drop down to the swampy ground to the west (left) at the head of Jarvis Clough. Go down this delightful clough, keeping to the true left bank and very shortly you cross the Lady Bower Brook and climb the few feet to the Sheffield–Glossop road (A57). This is one of the only two main roads you cross on this route – you cross this again later at the top of the Snake Road on Featherbed Moss and the A6013 is crossed near Yorkshire Bridge towards the end of the day.

Across the road is an old quarry and the way lies up through the trees overshadowing it. Out onto the slope of open moor now, walking north and making for the first gritstone tor of **Derwent Edge**. If the pace has been fast this outcrop, Whinstone Lee Tor (map reference: 200/877) will be gained in a little over an hour from Overstones Farm. Continue north along the edge, past the Hurkling Stones, the conspicuous coach and horse-like Wheel Stones, White Tor, the Grimmsian Salt Cellar (where more than one climber has been temporarily marooned) and so to the 1656 foot (504 metre) Dovestone Tor. You are now on National Trust property and on a clear day can look down to the south-west to Mill Brook and the fragments of Derwent village on the edge of the reservoir.

Dovestone Tor is the highest point on the actual face of Derwent Edge, which does not extend any farther north than the lowest point of the saddle between Dovestone Tor and Back Tor. It appears the craggiest and loftiest summit on the whole 'range' when seen from the other side of Derwent Dale but is actually 109 feet (33 metres) lower than more remote Back Tor, which you see rising ahead as you continue by the comical triple-tor of the Cakes of Bread, over to the east of your route.

Just beyond these rocks you cross the old Foulstone Road, a track over the watershed between Foulstone Delf in Bradfield Dale and Derwent Dale. You are walking along the South Yorkshire–Derbyshire county boundary here, though soon it swings off to the west. A mile (1.5 km) north of Dovestone Tor you gain the summit of Back Tor (1765 feet/ 538 metres). G.H.B. Ward's description of the place cannot be bettered:

The wind is always blowing as you sit on the cairn on the topmost slanting rock of Back Tor, and a more empty, homeless scene you cannot find. It is a fitting region for creatures that love loneliness; and you have them near. The curlew calls plaintively across the marshy cloughs. The gun-surviving hawk sails past on easy wing scanning the great hillsides, and the plover wails from the fields that edge the moor below. A hare, startled from amid the rocks, darts off in a straight line, trusting only to its speed, terrified by the unusual sight of man. It is a

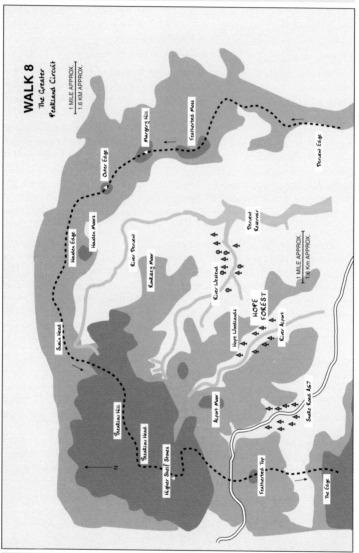

WALK 8
The Greater
Peakland Circuit

1 MILE APPROX.
1.6 KM APPROX.

Margery Hill

Featherbed Moss

Outer Edge

Derwent Edge

Howden Edge

Howden Moor

River Derwent

Ronksley Moor

Swain Head

Derwent Reservoir

River Westend

Hope Woodlands

HOPE
FOREST

River Ashop

Airport

Bleaklow Hill

Bleaklow Head

Airport Moor

Snake Road A57

Higher Shelf Stones

Featherbed Top

The Edge

N

1 MILE APPROX.
1.6 Km APPROX.

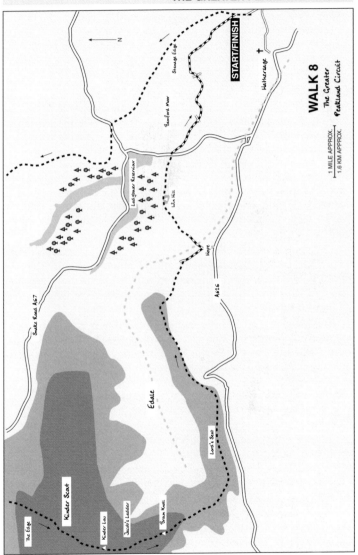

START/FINISH

N

Stanage Edge

Hathersage +

Bamford Moor

Ladybower Reservoir

Win Hill

Hope

A625

Swains Road A67

Edale

Lord's Seat

The Edge

Kinder Scout

Kinder Low

Jacob's Ladder

Brown Knoll

WALK 8

The Greater
Peakland Circuit

1 MILE APPROX.
1.6 KM APPROX.

wild, wide place, far from the ways of men, who here are the most occasional of creatures, and all its notes have the sadness of great spaces – of the mountains, moors, and seas. And yet it does one good to get into this upland, age-long solitude, where the primeval world is felt to be a mighty fact, linked to us. The spirit of the moors has his throne on Back Tor.

It is worthwhile to look round and study the district. The Mam Tor range is dwarfed by the long ridge of the Kinderscout plateau, which from here looks one high continuous level till it is suddenly cut off and drops to the Snake at Fairbrook Naze. That ragged end is the hill of the whole scene. To the right of Kinder there is trenched valley beyond trenched valley up to Bleaklow; and more to the right not only do the continuatory ridges to the one on which you stand – Howden Edge, Wilfrey Edge, and Margery Hill – stand out clear and high as yourself, but the scene is backed up by Black Hill (1908 feet/582 metres) on the north of Longdendale.

On again, over **Margery Hill** and across Cut Gate to **Outer Edge** (map reference: 177/970) where the ground around is lit by a sea of the purest white of cloudberry blooms in early summer. You have now walked 11¼ miles (17.5 km) and this should have taken no more than 3¾ hours if you are to complete the route before nightfall.

The loneliest and perhaps the hardest section of the walk is now followed. Keeping to the indistinct watershed, **Howden Edge** is crossed, over Featherbed Moss to **Swains Head**. Crossing the county boundary here you are back inside Derbyshire, where you will remain for the rest of the day. Bear round to the south now, with Swains Greave low on the left. A rough pull up to 2060 feet (633 metres) above sea level brings you onto Bleaklow Stones, the easternmost of the three principal tops of Bleaklow.

In poor visibility the route-finding will keep you fully occupied, but on a clear day the long, swelling summit ridge of the massif is seen far to the west. Walk now west for almost 2 miles (3 km) along the highest ridge of what constitutes Britain's only true desert.

Along the watershed are the rotting stakes marking the parish boundaries and these are sometimes a help to route-finding in bad weather. Here and there, as on the top of **Bleaklow Hill**, the horizon is broken by upstanding tors, remnants of a higher gritstone skyline. Around these

Kinder Scout and Derwent Dale from the Salt Cellar, Derwent Edge

tors are the gravelly remains of their once-larger selves. Erosion by wind, frost and acid rain is manifest up here among the mountain hares and curlews and grouse. The peat cover is also being removed and the bare gritstone beneath is showing through, while the flora has been influenced – *Nardus stricta* (white bent) in association with bilberry and heather is colonising what was once an area of cotton grass cover.

At **Bleaklow Head** you can look down to the north-west, to the upper reaches of Torside Clough with the enigmatic mound of Torside Castle a little over 1 mile (1.5 km) distant. Turn south now to **Higher Shelf Stones** (2039 feet/621 metres) and admire the views in every direction if the conditions allow (see Walk 4). The walk across Bleaklow took me almost 35 minutes of fast going. Then go down over Gathering Hill, across Crooked Clough, the Devils Dyke and the paved section of Doctor's Gate (see Walk 9) to the 1680 foot (512 metre) top of the Snake Road.

Head for the 1785 foot (544 metre) **Featherbed Top** (map reference: 091/921) and so on down Upper Gate Clough to Ashop Clough. I had a quick lunch, setting off again south at 12.40pm up the steep heather of

Black Ashop Moor and on to **The Edge** (the north-facing edge of Kinder Scout) near Spot Height 2049 feet (625 metres) and on to the south-west to Kinder Gates (map reference: 086/888). This is the oft-dramatic gritstone gateway through which the River Kinder flows on its way to the leap down Kinder Downfall.

Now make for the trig point on **Kinder Low** at 2077 feet (633 metres) and so down the peaty slopes to Edale Cross (map reference: 081/861). The walk from Ashop Clough to Edale Cross took me 1¼ hours, largely due to the misleadingly difficult nature of a crossing of this sector of the plateau – it is wide from north to south here.

South-south-eastwards to the tussock-topped **Brown Knoll**, along Colbourne and over Chapel Gate (the ancient trackway between Edale and Chapel-en-le-Frith) onto **Lord's Seat**. In less than 1 mile (2.5 km) to the east Mam Tor's top is reached. It was 3.45pm when I gained this summit. Now the route follows the Great Ridge, over Back Tor and Lose Hill (where there is a viewfinder in memory of G.H.B. Ward) and so down steep grass to the River Noe (map reference: 168/845).

A rest down here among the trees is followed by the stiff climb up the slope to Hope Brink and more easily east to the capping gritstone of **Win Hill**'s 1523 foot (462 metre) summit. Then down, still eastwards, through the steep woods to the Derwent at Yorkshire Bridge (map reference: 198/850), reached in an hour from leaving the Noe. Go up the lane to the main Bamford–Ladybower road – the third and last main road to be crossed on this walk – and up the steep lane under Bamford Edge, by Bole Hill, Dennis Knoll and Sheepwash Bank. This last section, from Yorkshire Bridge, is all of 5 miles (8 km) of steady, uphill going and at the end of a long day seems almost endless.

And then there is the last turn of the lane by the plantation (map reference: 240/836) and ½ mile (0.75 km) of uphill straight to your starting point. The light was pale when I arrived there.

To make the walk a round 50 miles (80 km) I would suggest that you walk south-west from the top of the Snake Road, over Moss Castle to Mill Hill (map reference: 062/904) and then up the ridge leading to Spot Height 2031 feet (624 metres) (map reference: 077/895), and so to Kinder Gates. From Edale Cross you would detour again, to the south-west and along the long spur of upland extending to South Head and Mount Famine (map reference 055/849), then return along this ridge, over Spot Height 1604 feet (494 metres) to Brown Knoll and so south along the original route.

Not to set any records but simply to indicate the sort of pace required to undertake and complete this walk comfortably, I would point out that I needed 14 hours 50 minutes to cover the 42 miles (67 km), an average speed of almost 3 miles (4.8 km) per hour, including all stops.

This route is unique in that it remains at a high level and away from habitation for much of its distance and is in the true traditions of the 'bog trotting' fraternity.

WALK 9

Along the Roman Road from Melandra to Brough

Outline:-	**Old Glossop, Mossylee, Doctor's Gate, Woodlands Valley, Hope Cross, Hope**
Map:-	**OS 1:25,000 Outdoor Leisure Sheet 1 'The Peak District – Dark Peak Area'**
Distance:	**15 miles/24 km**
Parking:	**Gamesley or Glossop town centre**

Melandra still exists, a ruin by the meanders of the moor-born Etherow south of the main road through Dinting Vale, west of Glossop. Navio, the Roman fort in the Hope Valley, has gone from the surface it once proudly surveyed from its Noe-side bank, where the small Bradwell Brook swirls in. In the last century excavations have uncovered many interesting objects, clarifying the position as regards Roman occupation and life in Peakland 2000 years ago. Many of the finds of Navio are to be seen in the Borough Museum at Buxton. Brough is situated at a little over 500 feet (152 metres) at the confluence of the Noe with Bradwell Brook, a thriving little hamlet, typical of many in this region. Because Navio's remains are so near to Brough I have entitled this walk '...from Melandra to Brough'.

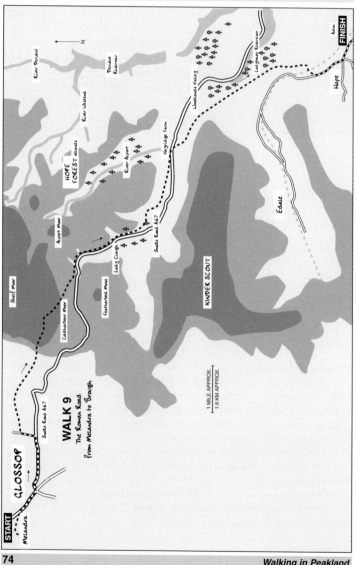

START
Melandra

GLOSSOP

Snake Road A57

WALK 9
The Roman Road
from Melandra to Brough

Snake Road A57

Cadishead Moor

Shelf Moor

Featherbed Moss

Lady Clough

Airport Moor

Snake Road A57

HOPE
FOREST Woods

River Ashop

River Ashop

Hagy Lidge Farm

KINDER SCOUT

EDALE

River Derwent

Derwent
Reservoir

River Westend

Woodlands Valley

Ladybower Reservoir

Hope

Aston

FINISH

N

1 MILE APPROX.
1.6 KM APPROX.

Route

Though it may be more convenient to walk the road in the reverse direction I have decided to give details starting at Melandra.

Glossop is a typically Lancastrian town, facing the flatter land of Greater Manchester, backing up the foothills of Pennine gritstone moorland. However, the old town is in Derbyshire, though it may seem to have few affinities in that direction.

Melandra's remains are about 1 mile (1.5 km) west of the town, 200 yards (180 metres) or so south-west of the A57 road where it used to be crossed by a bridge carrying a mineral line, and where the Etherow makes a large loop close to the left of the road. Here a lane takes you down on the left to **Melandra** (map reference: 009/951).

The best way from Melandra is back along the A57 into the centre of **Glossop**, making for Old Glossop on the north-eastern side of the present town centre. At the Domesday Survey, Glossop belonged to the Crown, then to William Pevril, the Crown again, the Abbey of Basingwerk, the Earl of Shrewsbury and, finally, the Duke of Norfolk obtained possession of the Manor Rolls. Seven centuries ago the name 'Glotsop' described its position very well, for it indeed occupied 'a small, enclosed valley overhanging another' (Old English: Glott's Hop – Glott's small, overhanging valley). Look at the position that Old Glossop occupies, at the mouth of the steep little valley of the Shelf Brook, murmuring down from the heights of Bleaklow's western fringe. The Roman way follows this valley initially.

In 800 yards (730 metres) Small Clough comes in from the left, draining part of Harrop Moss. On the right is tree-clad Shire Hill, just over 1000 feet (305 metres) high. Soon the rocky outcrops overlooking Yellowslacks Brook can be discerned, 1 mile (1.5 km) away, up on the left. Then there is Mossylee, a fine Peakland farm with sheep as its main concern. The high wall on the left should be noted, with its projecting layer of stones below the copings, the best deterrent for lively hill sheep. In front of Mossylee are banks of rhododendron, flanking a well-sited mill dam. In May and early June in most years the scattered hawthorns make great drifts across the grass, and the rhododendrons are like spilt blood beyond the water.

Follow the Shelf Brook, literally a 'shelf brook', for the gritstone has eroded along its bedding planes to make delightful steps, so often the case with carboniferous gritstone in the Pennines.

For most of 1½ miles (2.5 km) the track keeps not far from the brook, then a number of steep twists, a crossing of a crumpled gully and a final climb bring you onto the moaning top of **Coldharbour Moor** at 1650 feet (502 metres) above sea level.

There are 170 places named Coldharbour in England. It is unlikely that they were so designated because of the shelter they offered in cold weather as these placenames occur in both sheltered and bleak situations – there are 26 in Kent apparently. Most of these places are found in close proximity to Roman roads, and recent research suggests that the name comes from either 'calida arbor' (a warm tree) or from 'colubris arbor' (a place where the serpent standards of the Roman Legions were deposited – most likely at rest-houses by the military roads). Both suggestions seem possible, for a rest-house would have been likely at the top of the steep pull-up from the Shelf Valley.

In the winter the next ¾ mile (1.25 km) can be as wild as anywhere in our islands. Deep snow and swirling blizzards have meant the death of many men and animals in years gone by, not least in the packhorse days. What a task the Romans set themselves in connecting Melandra with their fort of Navio. There is not much to remind you of a typical Roman road on this route; the terrain did not allow the construction of many straight sections. But in the summer, especially the early summer, the cloudberries are banked about in the peaty groughs, small tortoise-shells dance from bilberry to tormentil and the young molinia grasses wave. Lying in the noon-sun upon a heather bank you can almost always watch a lark ascending or listen to a mayfly's lazy drone in June.

There are lively views backwards down the Shelf Brook Clough, and Kinder Scout's northern edge lies 2 miles (3.25 km) away southwards. The next section of the road is the best preserved, being paved and edged with uprights. It is between 3 and 4 feet wide (1 metre) and in a remarkable state of preservation. It is hard to believe that the stones have seen two millennia! After ½ mile (0.75 km) of pretty level going the track drops down to the comparative modernity of the Snake Pass, so named for the moors hereabouts have been owned by the Cavendish family for a long period, and the snake features prominently in that family's coat of arms. It was one of the last turnpikes to be built in this country, the lonely windings of Doctor's Gate (the paved section of the Roman way) being the only route across this col previously. Doctor's Gate? Yes, an enigmatic title for no-one has succeeded in tracing the identity of the

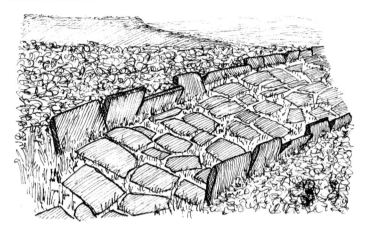

A detail of Doctor's Gate on Coldharbour Moor

doctor who gave his name to the Gate (old roadway). It has been suggested that there is a connection between it and Doctor Faust and the Devil but this has not been proven. William Senior's plans in Chatsworth refer to 'Doctor Talbot's gate' and Camden used the modern form of 'Doctor's Gate' in 1789.

The main road is followed now for a 1¾ miles (2.75 km) then, before the Snake Inn is reached on the left-hand, look for a stile into the spruce plantation on the left side of the road. Here the newer road leaves the ancient foundations and continues past the joining of **Lady Clough** and Ashop Clough and the Snake Inn *en route* for Sheffield. But you have not seen the last of this road; you cross it again 2 miles (3.25 km) lower down.

I always enjoy the next couple of miles (3.25 km), where the roadway meanders in and out, up and down, round a conifer's trunk and by a broken wall. If you watch carefully you will notice the crumbling face of Dinas Sitch Tor a few minutes after leaving the main road, half hidden in spruce, toppling down the steep on the left. What a strangely Welsh name this tor has, derived from the Old English sic, a small stream. There is a dampness here that explains how the tor got its name.

Soon the trees thin and you leave this section of Hope Forest. The bold gritstone contours lead the eye and leg into the mouth of Oyster Clough. What a strange fascination this valley has (see Walk 7)! The clough gets its name from the oyster-like opening of its contours above its narrow, gorge-like mouth, where its stream joins the mother Ashop near Upper House (map reference: 119/901).

Once across the brook into the clough bottom the route is clear, a slight rise up past the ruins of an old shooting cabin on the left. In the next 1½ miles (2.5 km) the old road follows a gradual descent which eventually crosses the main road again. Down on the right you will see the backs of Upper House and Wood House. Then the track enters a cutting, hedged with ancient hawthorns and soon you pass through the farmyard at **Hayridge Farm**, overlooking the mouth of the River Alport.

Turn left up the lane leading into the Alport Valley for a couple of hundred yards (185 metres) and then turn down the pasture on the right, over a stile and down through a handful of lovely beech, birch and rowan to the road bridge over the Alport. There is a footpath signpost here.

By walking back up the main road for a few yards you will see a clump of shrubs on the left-hand side, over the wall. These hide the mouth of a tunnel built over a century ago by a local farmer who had the idea of bringing water from the River Alport to drive a mill (see 'In Alport Dale').

Go back down the road, rightwards down to the actual confluence of the Alport with the Ashop and over the footbridge to the far bank. The track has always forded the river here but pedestrians can now walk across dry-shod. Follow the sunken lane up to a gate, where you will see Upper Ashop Farm standing back to the right, rather bleak and bare and typical of a Pennine gritstone farm. The road beyond the farm is properly made and leads on down and across the Ashop, joining the Snake Road below Rowlee Farm. The Roman road forks up to the right, climbing ever steeper and with improving views over the Woodlands Valley. The eastern vista becomes clearer, of Hallam Moors and Derwent Edge and the suggestion of desert and sky over to the north. This steep section always seems long to me, perhaps because it usually comes at the end of a long day. This is not the actual Roman road but a medieval trackway, the original route being some yards to the right, further into the hillside; as careful searching will reveal.

A levelling of the way, through a gate and over the little stream draining Blackley Clough. The stepping stones here invariably give trouble; wet feet and mud splatters!

A little over ½ mile (0.75 km) beyond Blackley Clough the gaunt stone pillar called Hope Cross is approached. There is a cross-roads here, a four-lane-ends of great antiquity. The date 1737 is not the date of erection of the pillar; it is much older than that. It probably takes the place of an even older marker across this windswept saddle between Win Hill and the bold brow of Crookstone Knoll (1710 feet/521 metres), easternmost corner of Kinder Scout's perimeter. No doubt the road was better used a few centuries ago, by general travellers and packhorse trains – lead from Castleton and Bradwell, wool from the remote farms, and livestock bound for market. The four sides state 'Sheffield', 'Edale', 'Hope' and 'Glossop'. One name on each side.

On down towards Hope, along the wide, grassy track which gradually descends to the confines of the Edale Valley between Win and Lose Hills. Two miles (3.25 km) from the cross, the road takes a sharp right-hand turn by Fullwood Stile Farm, over the railway line and down to the Edale lane at Townhead. The old bridge and farm buildings make a sight quite different from those that have passed, deep green clough and moory waste, wild river's sweep and steep climb by broken walls. Here you can watch swallows nesting in an old barn in summer by the bridge and trout gliding under it.

On into **Hope** village. The church here can boast of being one of the oldest in northern Derbyshire, having been in existence with a priest at the Domesday Survey, though the present building was erected in the thirteenth century. It seems strange that the castle of Hope mentioned in the reign of Edward I is not there today, unless the remains of Castleton's Peveril Castle or Brough's Navio were mistakenly called Hope Castle.

Where the Edale Lane meets the A625 road by Hope church turn right, then left behind the church. Soon after crossing Peakshole Water (the stream coming down the valley from Castleton) take a lane forking to the left. A steep climb up over the 650 foot (198 metre) contour and ½ mile (0.75 km) after the last fork you will see the fields where Navio once stood.

I can do no better than refer the reader to Dr Mary Andrew's work 'Long Ago in Peakland', where you will be able to read in some detail of the excavations and discoveries at Navio in the twentieth century.

Three Hills and a River: the White Peak Area

The carboniferous limestone of the Peak District forms what is often referred to as the White or Low Peak. Only one walk (Walk 10) in this book is over the limestone of the National Park and that because it follows a Roman road of interest (Buxton to Brough). I have not described more walks which keep entirely to this limestone country for although I find the area fascinating from a historical and, occasionally, from a scenic point of view, I much prefer to walk upon the open country of the younger gritstone and the infinite variety of the bordering coal measures.

But this is not to ignore the White Peak altogether. On the western fringe are several features which are among the National Park's finest.

Of all the limestone hills the most beautiful trio are Chrome Hill, Parkhouse Hill and Thorpe Cloud. They overlook the River Dove on its true left bank, the first two not far below its source, the third 15 miles (24 km) further downstream.

Chrome and Parkhouse form a small range, together with Hollins Hill to the north-west and Hitter Hill, Aldery Cliff and High Wheeldon to the south-east. Earl Sterndale, about 4½ miles (7.25 km) south of Buxton, is the nearest village to this group of hills. I consider the best views of Chrome and Parkhouse to be from the steep slopes immediately eastward of the village while Chrome presents a most dramatic silhouette when seen from the crest of Axe Edge, 3 miles (4.75 km) to the north-west.

Both hills appear far bigger and higher than they are, a distortion due to a combination of their sharp shapes and isolated position above the Dove. They are superb examples of fossiliferous limestone reefs projecting through the surrounding shales. It is not hard to believe that they were formed by the accumulation of fossils in a warm sea long ago, before the younger grits and shales were deposited by river estuaries. These more recent deposits eventually covered the reefs. For unknown ages the superlative forms lay in the darkness under the newer rocks. Only the subsequent action of weathering has removed this latter material to reveal the reefs again. Continued activity on the part of frost, rain, wind and sun had dramatised their profiles – a process which is still going on. It is an interesting exercise to imagine what these twin hills will look like in another 5000 years!

From Earl Sterndale church (map reference: 091/671) you can walk down to the inn and turn right towards the main Buxton–Longnor road (B5053) and turn left down towards Longnor for ¼ mile (0.5 km) to Glutton Farm (map reference: 084/671). You are virtually at the foot of the east ridge of Parkhouse Hill here and it is a simple matter to walk up the steep, scrub-dotted slope to the sharp, white crest. Chrome Hill appears near to the west, and the smooth slopes of the upper Dove Valley lie below to the south. You are little more than 1100 feet (335 metres) above sea level. Then drop down the steep and stony west ridge into Dowel Dale.

Farther up this limestone dale are numerous caves where prehistoric man lived and his remains are now giving scope to the archaeologist's explorations. Continuing slightly north of west you are quickly upon Chrome's east ridge and when the top is reached you are just over 1200 feet (365 metres) above sea level. Among the broken reef rocks of Chrome is a cavern called the Devil's House and Parlour. An old tradition states that the Devil came here to hang himself but did not manage it, so he haunts the hill-top daily from midnight to dawn.

The 1274 foot (388 metre) high Hollins Hill rises to the north-west but this is not so beautiful of shape, though a burial mound on the summit is an object of encouragement to climb.

From the top of both Chrome Hill and Parkhouse Hill the western horizon is shadowed by the graceful gritstone eminencies of the West Moor – Morridge, Oliver Hill and Axe Edge. If you decide to walk that way one of the best routes is to cross the Dove to Hollinsclough hamlet (map reference: 065/666). Less than 1 mile (1.5 km) to the south-east of this place, by the lane to Longnor, is Moss Carr. This is a peat bog boasting a very rich flora. If time allows you should go there, especially in late spring or summer. In this low, wet area the bogbean (*Menyanthes trifoliata*) still flourishes, as does marsh cinquefoil (*Potentilla palustris*), spotted orchid (*Dactylorchis maculata subsp. ericetorum*) and the dwarf purple orchid (*Orchis purpurella*), the latter only discovered here since the middle of the twentieth century.

This is, of course, one of the major attractions of the limestone country. The flora of the carboniferous limestone of the Peak District is very varied and in early summer especially you can spend many happy hours discovering many flowering species in the delicate colouring of the deeper dales and on the hill slopes.

Then go up the steep lane from Moss Carr for almost 3 miles (4.5 km) beyond Hollinsclough to the Leek–Buxton road (A53) close to Flash Head. Just down to the left (south) before the main road is reached is a damp hollow. In this the River Manifold is born, in this district called Flash Head.

Continuing northwards along the main road for ½ mile (0.75 km) a farmhouse is reached, standing on the left-hand side of the road. Over the front door is carved 'Dove Head' and if you look down the field on the right-hand side of the road (just opposite the farmhouse) you will notice a stone-flagged path leading diagonally to the corner of the field. Take this clean and well-set slabbed path which leads to a spring in a few yards. This is the source of the world-famous River Dove, or so most people agree. There are a few who do not, and would assign the source to a rushy moor-stream which rises near the top of Axe Edge 1 mile (1.5 km) to the north, but tradition firmly asserts this to be the source.

Now look at the slab on the top of the stone trough. On it are carved the interlocking initials of Izaak Walton and Charles Cotton. These notable angling partners are said to have followed their beloved river to its source and on finding the Springs of Dove carved their initials on the slab over the source. However, the carving is less than 150 years old and as Walton died in 1683 and Cotton in 1687 the story cannot be true; in fact, a skilled stone-mason executed the carving, with more than a touch of romanticism. In 1903 the stone was cracked by a hard frost but this has not spoilt the actual initials.

A little to the north of Dove Head the road can be left and Axe Edge ascended. The first top is just over 1800 feet (548 metres) above sea level and 1 mile (1.5 km) northward walking over tussock grass brings you to the 1810 foot (551 metre) top of the edge. On a clear day the views are extensive.

Eight hundred feet (243 metres) below to the north-east is Buxton with the great bulk of Combs Moss and distant Ladder Hill behind; and behind Combs Moss the mass of Kinder Scout leads to the hills of the north. Round the western horizon as the eye swings are Shining Tor – 24 feet (7 metres) higher than your viewpoint – the Cat and Fiddle, the

*Dove Head below Axe Edge and the monogram formed by the
initials of Isaac Walton and Charles Cotton above the spring*

summit of Shutlingsloe looking very big, and the dip slope of the
Roaches. To the south-east are the green and swelling vales of the
Manifold and the Dove, then smooth Hollins Hill and Chrome Hill –
looking for all the world like a miniature Pumori. Away to the east the
tree-topped ridges of the limestone land fade into vagueness.

The River Dove forms the border between Derbyshire and
Staffordshire for its entire length from Dove Head to its confluence with
the Trent near Burton-upon-Trent (with a few slight deviations southwards from Rocester). Thirteen and a half miles (21.5 km) downstream
from Chrome and Parkhouse that third notable limestone hill comes into
view round a deeply-wooded bend in Dovedale.

Thorpe Cloud, too, is a reef knoll, a prominent monument to the
carboniferous age, having weathered less rapidly than the surrounding
limestone. It is lower than the former pair, its top being only 942 feet
(287 metres) above sea level; though it is not less imposing for this.

From the village of Thorpe the Cloud (map reference: 152/510) is easily climbed. Upon reaching the top you will at once see what a commanding position it holds as a sentinel to Dovedale's southern mouth. It really forms the eastern gatepost to the Dale – Bunster Hill forms the western gatepost. The Dale appears directly below as you peer from the white crest. The Cloud's most noble profile is seen from the vicinity of the Peveril of the Peak Hotel.

I once went up Thorpe Cloud at sunset and watched the brilliant banners fade beyond the gritstone rim of West Moor, somewhere beyond the Roaches. The sheep were my only companions in the warm night.

WALK 10

Along the Roman Road from Buxton to Brough

Outline:	Buxton, Fairfield Common, Peak Dale, Bradwell Moor, Smalldale, Brough
Map:	OS 1:25,000 Outdoor Leisure Sheet 1 'The Peak District – Dark Peak Area'; OS 1:25,000 Outdoor Leisure 24 'The Peak District – White Peak Area'
Distance:	11 miles/17.5 km
Parking:	Buxton town centre

Besides the route from Melandra to Brough (Navio) the Romans built a road between Buxton (Aquae Arnemetiae) and Little Chester, near Derby; a road between Brough and Templeborough, near Rotherham; and a shorter route connecting Brough with Buxton (at that time a spa where the Roman overlords rested and recuperated assisted by the warm mineral waters there – mineral waters which still run today).

Route

For convenience this walk is described from Buxton to Brough, though it could be reversed and so come as a suitable ending to Walk 9, following the Roman route from Melandra to Aquae Arnemetiae via Navio.

From the railway viaduct over the eastern end of Spring Gardens in **Buxton** walk up Fairfield Road, passing the thirteenth-century St Peter's church on the left. Proceed along the A6 road (towards Chapel-en-le-Frith) across Fairfield Common for 1½ miles (2.5 km), turning off to the right at this distance (map reference: 074/757).

This is Batham Gate, the line of the original Roman road across the often-bleak limestone upland between Buxton and the Derwent Valley. You follow this general north-easterly-pointing direction all the way to Brough now. In less than 1 mile (1.5 km) the road rises to the cross-roads on top of Longridge, then down ½ mile (0.75 km) into **Peak Dale** village, at 1000 feet (304 metres) above sea level. And just beyond this

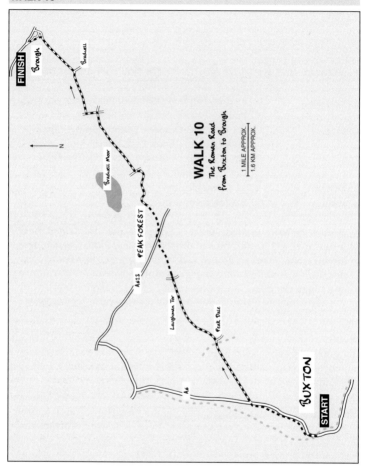

WALK 10
The Roman Road
from Buxton to Brough

1 MILE APPROX.
1.6 KM APPROX.

FINISH — Brough, Bradwell, Bradwell Moor, PEAK FOREST, A623, Laughman Tor, Peak Dale, BUXTON — START

← N

you cross over the old Manchester–London railway line of the former Midland Railway via Derby.

This Peak Dale area must be one of the ugliest and least interesting places in the entire Peak District – it was no accident that caused the

National Park boundary to circumnavigate this whole 'Quarry World' of Dove Holes, Peak Dale, Great Rocks Dale and Harpurhill!

Up the hill beyond the railway and on through pleasant Smalldale. This is a hamlet of ancient farms and more recent quarrymen's homes. Carry on up the lane now, and very soon you come to the top of the hill to see a vast limestone bowl stretching to the north and east, a bowl of pasture fields and neat deciduous copses. The village of **Peak Forest** stands in the centre of this hollow, with the high shoulder of Bradwell Moor rising to 1500 feet (457 metres) behind. This bowl-sited village was once a clearing at the heart of the old Peak Forest, a natural Royal Forest of Norman kings and their successors.

Soon after passing a rectangular wood of sycamores on the right you join the road between Peak Forest and Wormhill at right-angles (map reference: 111/783). Go over the stile in the wall ahead and so across eight fields to the conspicuous S-bend on the Calver–Chapel-en-le-Frith road (A623) far ahead. *En route* across the fields you drop into the head of Dam Dale and through the yard of the farm there. There is a most interesting walk up four dales (Monk's Dale, Peter Dale, Hay Dale and Dam Dale) from Miller's Dale to Peak Forest.

On gaining the main road at the S-bend walk uphill to the top right-hand bend and look back. You will see that this is a piece of the Roman route, continued 1 mile (1.5 km) away to the west, where you left the lane before crossing the fields. Now walk along the main road towards the south-east for 250 yards (230 metres).

Turn left towards **Bradwell** in front of a farmhouse, not long ago a public house. In ½ mile (0.75 km) the Roman road (Batham Gate) crosses obliquely (map reference: 132/791) but it is very indistinct here and therefore keep to the lane which swings to and fro. After crossing the line of the Roman road again (map reference: 135/793) look over the wall on the left to see the foundations of this original route, a long, raised, grassy mound running almost parallel with the lane. At the next corner there was a Roman camp, with earthworks still visible high up on the left-hand rise.

Quite soon at 1450 feet (442 metres), you turn sharp left for 100 yards (90 metres), then right. Again you have joined the Roman road and now you follow the straight, descending lane with its ancient foundation for 1½ miles (2.5 km), by a gravel quarry on Moss Rake to eventually join the Little Hucklow–Castleton road. Turn left for 250 yards (230 metres) then right down Batham Gate again.

Soon you are descending into Smalldale (another Smalldale) and past very old Smalldale Hall, half-hidden up on the left. And so down to the main road (B6049) between Bradwell and the Sheffield–Chapel-en-le-Frith road (A625) beyond Brough.

Continue along the main road to **Brough** village. It is 1 mile (1.5 km) down this road, and on the way you pass Cohort's Villa, a comparatively new dwelling with a name to remind you of long ago. A cohort was the tenth part of a Roman legion, containing three maniples or six centuries. Just before reaching Brough Mill (left side) a path leads up the grass slope towards Hope. At the centre of the second field are the only signs of Navio Roman fort, excavated early in the twentieth century but covered over with soil since.

Continue along this path to Hope village or go back to the road, pass Brough Mill and reach the Sheffield–Chapel-en-le-Frith road (A625) in 3 minutes (map reference: 184/827).

WALK 11

Ludworth Intakes, Lantern Pike and Chinley Churn

Outline:	Glossop, Coombes Tor, Robin Hood's Picking Rods, Ludworth Moor, Mellor Hall, Mellor, Mellor Moor, Aspenshaw Hall, Lantern Pike, Abbot's Chair, Monk's Road, Chunal, Glossop (or Lantern Pike, Birch Vale, Chinley Churn, Chinley)
Map:	OS 1:25,000 Outdoor Leisure Sheet 1 'The Peak District – Dark Peak Area'
Distance:	14½ miles/23 km
Parking:	Glossop town centre or Charlestown (Map ref: 034/929)

These walks cover the western slopes of Peakland, a region dissimilar to the rest of the National Park and its fringes. The hills, the valley, the farms, the entire atmosphere seem different from any other district I know; not as wild as the heights of the highest Peak, and not as green and quiet and protected as those valleys of the eastern margin. These western slopes occupy a place between the wilderness of the highest tops and the placid eastern vales. A high hill like Shutlingsloe is a rugged, exposed place but is surrounded by deep, wooded hollows like the Dane Valley which temper the general rugosity and the result is a district of charm and attraction. This first western walk is in the north and is probably bleaker of aspect than the remainder.

Route

We start in Glossop. Make for Charlestown (map reference: 034/929) and go up the lane past **Lees Hall** (map reference: 032/927) passing a filled-in quarry on the right and the open drop below the lane on the left. Where the National Park is entered at a steep, left-hand bend in

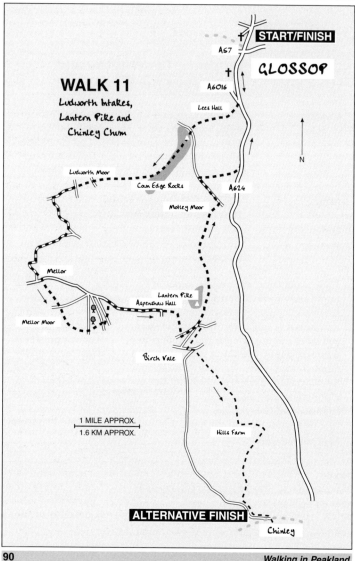

WALK 11
Ludworth Intakes,
Lantern Pike and
Chinley Churn

START/FINISH

GLOSSOP

A57

A6016

Lees Hall

A624

Ludworth Moor

Cown Edge Rocks

Motley Moor

N

Mellor

Lantern Pike

Aspenshaw Hall

Mellor Moor

Birch Vale

1 MILE APPROX.
1.6 KM APPROX.

Hills Farm

ALTERNATIVE FINISH

Chinley

the now-rough track, cut up the rough pasture ahead and over two further fields to the edge of Whiteley Nab. (Alternatively, continue up the lane in front of ancient Herod Farm and so up the grassy hollow to Whiteley Nab.) Once over the last field boundary and at the edge of the moorland turn left, noticing the wide backward views over Glossop's industry, and the fields and hills rising up to the television mast on Holme Moss.

In 5 minutes a stile in the wall is reached with the outcrop of **Cown Edge Rocks** beyond, topped by the trig point at 1300 feet (396 metres). Once the road is reached turn right for a short way until a stile is climbed over the left-hand wall. Up onto the moor you go, past the trig point with a wonderful 360-degree vista of north-western Peakland.

Over 5 miles (8 km) to the south-east is the double top of South Head and Mount Famine, rising in a steady spur to Brown Knoll and the Kinder massif. Due westwards, to the right of copse-topped Ludworth Intakes, the plain of south Lancashire and northern Cheshire stretches away to the Mersey.

Now you walk south-west over the open pasture for almost 1 mile (1.6 km). Where a grass track cuts across at right-angles and there is a good view of Kinder Scout's northern flank, turn right upon this track and down towards Far Slack Farm. Keeping along the wall dividing farmland from moor you pass a stone's throw from this lonely holding where the wind always seems to be blowing. At the next gateway are Robin Hood's Picking Rods (map reference: 006/909).

One authority considers these two stone pillars set in their stone sockets the place where local men 'picked' their future wives from the assembled maidens. That would certainly explain the odd name, but it would seem that the original purpose for which the Picking Rods were erected was more utilitarian. There is a very similar structure standing in a similar situation on Park Moor, 6 miles (9.5 km) to the south, called the Bow Stones (see Walk 13), and the name of this suggests an explanation. Bow Stones – something to do with archery. This whole area was covered by the Royal Forest of the Peak in Norman and later times and it is not unlikely that these twin pillars were used to bend a bow in order to string it. Once strung the bow could be lifted over the stone around which it had been levered. The scattered woodland of the Royal Forest extended over all the surrounding hilltops and upon two of them at least

Robin Hood's Picking Rods

these aids to archery were placed, for wild boar, deer, even wolves, roamed hereabouts until quite a late date.

Continue west, keeping along the wall-side, and aim for the copse upon **Ludworth** Intakes. Walk down the rough lane to the tarmac road from Chisworth to Rowarth. Cross this and so pass over an area of derelict land, by a quarry and along a track to the secondary road from Chisworth to Marple. Keep to the left, along the lane, for ½ mile (0.75 km) with ever more open views to the west and the sheltering shoulder of Ludworth Intakes up to the north.

This elevated area (reaching 958 feet/291 metres at Stirrup Benches) is so named for having been won from moorland – 'taken-in' to form properly cultivated and cared-for farmland – by the graver (a man who broke up moorland prior to cultivation with his graving spade) and his mate, the putter-over (who pulled over the sods with his mattock). There are many 'intakes' in the north of England, all formerly rough land which was later 'taken-in'.

Turn left down the first lane, Smithy Lane, into the valley bottom and up the rough, damp section to the Rowarth–Marple Bridge road. Turn up right towards Marple Bridge, through the group of farms and cottages ahead called Stonyford and where there is a sharp right turn keep straight on along the rough track ahead.

There is again an ever-widening view west over north-east Cheshire and the River Goyt. Very soon you pass on the north side of lovely old **Mellor** Hall ('IC 1691' set in one wall) with its well-preserved farm buildings (one barn has 'IC 1688' set in a wall and suggests that the hall is older than the first date suggests), and so down the neat drive and into the lane to Mellor church.

This is the parish church of St Thomas, standing proudly at 800 feet (243 metres) above sea level on its hill-end site and looking over the western plain beneath. The tower dates from AD1136 and the pulpit is the oldest in England, being carved from a solid block of wood between AD1330 and 1340. In the churchyard is a sundial made from the lower part of the ancient village cross; the old stocks and whipping post are still extant.

Down the hill keep left down the old, unmade road, noticing the

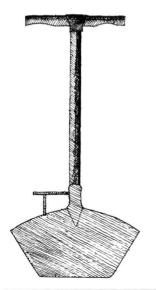

old wall stones tilted against the walls to prevent cartwheels catching in former times. Soon you climb to the Marple Bridge–New Mills road and turn left for 50 yards (45 metres). Immediately past the first group of cottages on the right hand turn up, beside these cottages, and so up a field path to Birchenough Farm (map reference: 990/880). You go through the yard here and then along the lane for almost 600 yards (549 metres) to the second junction on **Mellor Moor**.

Here you are a little over 1000 feet (304 metres) above sea level and in the left-hand wall is the remains of an ancient cross. Ahead is the

A graver's spade, used in the conversion of moorland to farmland

south-facing land called Napkin Piece. To the east is the long western face of Kinder Scout with the Downfall visible. Chinley Churn lies ahead as you walk down through Napkin Piece and there is an unusual view of the upper Goyt Valley and its reservoirs, with Combs Moss and Axe Edge distantly behind them.

Suddenly, down below, is the industrial curve of New Mills, Birch Vale and Hayfield. Continue directly down the lane to the Marple Bridge–New Mills road (map reference: 001/875). Turn right down the road and in 100 yards (90 metres) turn left down an old lane which slants on to Briergrove Farm. Turn right here, steeply down, passing the unique and tall-walled Blake Hall and so up the hill through a wooded glade to **Aspenshaw Hall**. This is an elegant house, contrasting with the wilder, strictly functional farmhouses passed so far on this walk.

The hard road soon ends at the next farm but you continue up what is now a bridle track. Here sallow and willow choke the way and you may see the local wrens busy in spring and summer. In May wood sorrel lies in white patches out of the wind like strewn blossom beneath crab apple trees.

When the Rowarth–Hayfield lane is gained ½ mile (0.75 km) above Aspenshaw Hall turn right and follow on round the contours to the first cross-lanes (map reference: 024/874). You have traversed around the south-western flank of Lantern Pike, and now turn up left to the scattered farms at Cliff.

At the end of this lane we enter the National Trust property which includes the top of **Lantern Pike**. Viewed from many sides this hill looks very ordinary but I would definitely advise anyone near the place to climb to the summit.

Lantern Pike truly dominates little Hayfield, as everyone who has looked down from its top will agree. Though under 1200 feet (365 metres) above sea level the views on clear days are remarkable. A view indicator was erected here in 1950 (like the one on Lose Hill's summit) to the memory of Edwin Royce (1880–1946) in recognition of his efforts to gain freedom for our hills. Northwich can be picked out 25 miles (40 km) to the west-south-west when the atmosphere is favourable.

From the top, one route takes you back by Cliff to **Birch Vale** and over Chinley Churn via Ollersett and Throstle Bank to **Chinley**. The other route, making the walk a circuit, takes you north-east from Lantern Pike's summit and onto the footpath below. As you go notice Park Hall in its secluding trees above Hayfield.

Park Hall was the home of Captain Jack White (1791–1866), son of a wealthy Manchester doctor. This character was one of the finest English horsemen during the first half of the nineteenth century and though a first-rate steeple-chaser, he was best known for endurance, it being recorded that he hunted 160 miles (256 km) on horse-back on one winter's day alone. Master of the Cheshire Hunt for 12 years, Captain Jack White never retired from the sporting saddle, despite many serious accidents – as when his horse fell on top of him in a ditch, smashing many of his bones.

Continue across the rough grassland to Blackshaw Farm, the nearest of four farms forming a square. Near Blackshaw Farm take the lane ahead (towards **Matley Moor**) and at the second farm – Matley Moor Farm – turn right and soon up left for ⅔ mile (1 km) to the Monk's Road (crossed earlier in the day). Turn right here and in 30 yards (27 metres) you reach a wide and grassy common on the right hand. In the farthest corner beneath an alpine-style wayside shrine is the ancient Abbot's Chair. There is little doubt that this hollowed-out stone got its name from association with the Monk's Road. It is of unknown origin though it may have been the base for a stone boundary pillar on this high ridge, with one side of the original socket broken away and now forming the 'chair'.

Having seen this turn back left along the Monk's Road for ½ mile (0.75 km) to Plainsteads (map reference: 025/911). Immediately behind the farm a narrow walled trackway takes you down into pretty Long Clough and up the other side to the main road (A624) just south of Chunal (map reference: 034/915). In a little over 1 mile (1.6 km) northwards down the main road you come easily to Charlestown and **Glossop**.

This has been an unusual walk in a comparatively unknown corner of Peakland. You can return here time after time and discover new walks and new details of this neglected countryside.

Cheshire's Share of the Peak Park

Some of the most beautiful and romantic countryside of the Peak District National Park is found outside Derbyshire, to the west, in eastern Cheshire. What is more charming than the deep, wooded slits of valley near Bosley Minn and Wincle Minn, more mysterious than the shadowed green of Macclesfield Forest or breezier than the top of Sponds Hill?

Lyme Hall stands in its park, extensive and wooded, south of Disley. The Legh family lived here for 600 years until 1946, when Robert Legh gave the hall and park to the National Trust. Not least attractive here are the red deer which inhabit the deep woods of the park, and the two sequoia trees by the car park below the hall. If, on a clear day, you walk through the woods and up on the open moor to Bowstonegate, the conspicuous farm atop the 1250 foot (381 metre) ridge running to Sponds Hill by an ancient trackway, the whole of the western Peak Park will be revealed. Grey folds and green dales, sheep calls and curlews and the distant line of the Cheshire Plain drawing your eye to the west. Look down to the south-east and you will see the valley (more correctly the clough) of the Todd Brook. Down there is pretty Kettleshulme, village of gardens and pride on the Whaley Bridge–Macclesfield road, the road which crosses the Todd Brook by Reed Bridge. This single span of gritstone is one of the most beautiful bridges I know and deserves examination. From Kettleshulme you can walk southwards up the steepish lane to Five Lane Ends, near the former Windgather Youth Hostel.

Up to the east, across a rough pasture field, are Windgather Rocks. This gritstone outcrop is ideal for learning the arts of cragmanship and as a result has been popular with weekend climbers for years. From the top of the Rocks you get a really fine impression of the parallel, westward-facing escarpments of this outlying Pennine area: a moorland dip slopes eastwards to the trough of the Goyt Valley and a steeper drop westwards to the headwaters of Todd Brook, with another eastward-facing dip slope up to Pike Low and Charles Head.

From Windgather you can walk due south for miles – along the top of this gritstone escarpment which is the Cheshire–Derbyshire boundary for over 3 miles – over Oldgate Nick, Cats Tor and Shining Tor (at 1834 feet/559 metres the highest point in Cheshire).

View north-east to Roych Clough and Lord's Seat from Eccles Pike (Walk 12)

The Dane Valley looking north-east to Tagsclough Hill (Walk 15)

Sunset on Shutlingsloe from the north (Walk 16)

After crossing the Macclesfield–Buxton road (A537) 1 mile (1.6 km) below the Cat and Fiddle Inn (second-highest licensed house in England) take the steep land down into Wildboarclough. This meandering clough is definitely one of my favourite valleys, with the most beautiful of all Peakland hills looking down – but more of that in a moment.

At the bottom of the hill there is a fork in the road, by the Stanley Arms, and this is Bottom-of-the-Oven – a lovely hamlet with a lovely name. Up on the brow of Toot Hill at 1300 feet (396 metres) is Forest Chapel, another village, but this time on top of a broad ridge. A handful of farms, a school and the parish church of St Stephen look down to the west towards the Bollin Valley and Macclesfield and the plain. The entire westward slope from Forest Chapel down to the Bollin Valley bottom is afforested – dense coniferous forest planted on part of what was once a royal forest set aside as a hunting ground under the Norman kings. Indeed, tradition has it that the last wild boar in England was killed in Wildboarclough. The forest was, of course, largely waste ground with only a thin woodland cover until the new forest was planted.

Here, in the parish of Wildboarclough and Forest Chapel, is held the very ancient ceremony of rush bearing. Rushes are carried to the church, a relic of the days when straw or rushes were used as the floor covering.

Only 1½ miles (2.4 km) southwards (as the crow flies) is that favourite hill, Shutlingsloe. From every point of the compass this is a graceful thing, conical and tapering to the sky in such a way that it seems to be very, very high. My favourite Shutlingsloe profile is from Tagsclough Hill, to the south-east, 1½ miles (2.4 km) away from the summit and just above the Congleton–Buxton road (A54).

The view from the top reveals the infinities of the Cheshire Plain and, if you are lucky, the sparkles of a bejewelled sea off the Wirral. Eastwards you look down into Wildboarclough village, many-treed and backed by the Axe Edge moors and Danebower, the soft moss where that Cheshire river is born just under the sky.

The Dane dominates the rest of Cheshire-within-the-Park, forming the frontier with Staffordshire for over 12 miles (19 km) from its source to where it goes under the Macclesfield Canal near Bosley, on the Leek–Macclesfield road (A523).

Heavily shaded with deciduous trees, sessile oak and silver and hairy birch predominating, the dale winds down below the slope where mysterious Lud's Church lurks, but that is in Staffordshire and another story. The Dane continues on down by Wincle and under high and airy Danebridge, by trout pools and moss-draped boulders and so on by Bearda and Hollinhall, to receive the Shell Brook from the northern flanks, draining Bosley and Wincle Minns.

And ½ mile (0.75 km) west of the reception of the Shell Brook the young Dane flows out of the Peak Park before going under Hugbridge and out across the Plain.

Eccles Pike, Chinley Churn and Edale Cross

Outline:	Chinley, Eccles Pike, Bradshaw Hall, the Roosdyche, Chinley Churn, Sett Valley, Edale Cross, Edale
Map:	OS 1:25,000 Outdoor Leisure Sheet 1 'The Peak District – Dark Peak Area'
Distance:	16 miles/25.5 km
Parking:	Chinley village centre

Writing almost a century ago J.B. Firth bemoaned the fact that the lower Goyt Valley had been abandoned to industry and had lost its beauty. While this is largely true – think of the copses of mill chimneys around Whaley Bridge, Furness Vale and New Mills – the older industrialisation has mellowed somewhat into its surroundings and, besides this, there are still many square miles of unspoilt country in the vicinity; this walk will prove this admirably.

Route

From the centre of **Chinley** take the lane south to Whitehough, an old village (more like a hamlet) across the stream. Look at the old hall close to the right-hand side of the lane before the junction of the ways (map reference: 039/821) before continuing up the hill.

In ⅓ mile (0.5 km) a handful of jumbled cottages and farm buildings are reached on the right (map reference: 041/818). Go along the lane through this collection of habitations, crossing the hard lane to Eccles House and Gnat Hole. Walk up the steepening lane – a grass track now – and as you do so the north-eastern slopes of **Eccles Pike** rear ahead ever nearer. The top of this conical hill is National Trust property, and soon you can enjoy the very wide and varied views from the top, weather permitting.

The grassy track becomes a stiled footpath and by the time Lidgate is reached (on the Eccles Pike 'Ridgeway') you have ascended 350 feet

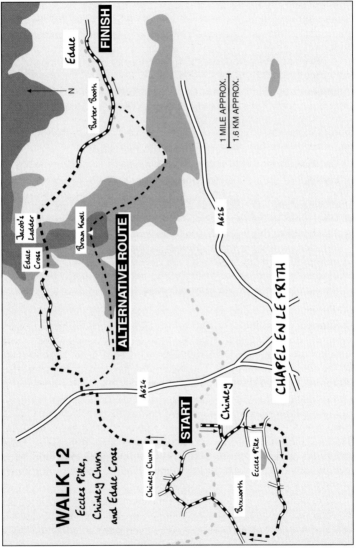

WALK 12
Eccles Pike,
Chinley Churn
and Edale Cross

FINISH

Edale

N

Burter Booth

Jacob's Ladder

Edale Cross

Brown Knoll

ALTERNATIVE ROUTE

1 MILE APPROX.
1.6 KM APPROX.

A615

A624

CHAPEL EN LE FRITH

START

Chinley

Chinley Churn

Eccles Pike

Buxworth

(106 metres) from the stream at Whitehough. Turn right up the lane and in less than ½ mile (0.75 km) the top of the hill is reached; the lane plunges on down to the west but you turn right through a gateway and so to the summit of the Pike (1213 feet/369 metres). On a clear day this is a viewpoint second to none for, though the vistas are not distant, you are placed centrally to look down on the Chinley, Goyt and Combs valleys. Beyond these green-and-smoky confines the gritstone hills rise steeply – Kinder Scout's western flanks to the north-east, Chinley Churn's tilt of rock and moor to the north, the graceful hills of the Cheshire border as far south as Shining Tor to the west, and Combs Moss and Black Edge rising to back the Combs Valley to the south.

Turn back to the road and retrace your steps to Lidgate. Immediately beyond the old farmhouse on the right take the footpath down towards Tunstead Milton and the Combs Valley. Go down through four fields, making for Bradshaw Hall as soon as the fourth field is reached. The path brings you into the yard above the Hall, by an unusual drystone-walled hollow through which a stream flows.

The well-proportioned Jacobean gateway carries the date 1620 and the name and arms of Francis Bradshaw. It is obvious that the old hall has seen better days – originally it was built in the shape of a cross and more than 100 years ago was redesigned internally to accommodate two families.

Walk on west between the farm buildings and on through three pasture fields, keeping along the same contour. An old farmhouse is now reached (map reference: 033/807) and you walk in front of this, up between the outbuildings and on up the old, grassy lane. The lane ends and you walk on diagonally to the left over two fields, where the Eccles Pike ('Ridgeway') lane is gained.

Turn left through the hamlet of Hilltop, noticing Ollerenshaw Hall (map reference: 026/808), a hall in complete contrast to the last one. This is a stately Georgian mansion, the result of the fortunes of an early local industrialist as against the less pretentious and more utilitarian building of a yeoman farmer of an earlier age. Walk on west down towards Over Leigh.

In Over Leigh you will hardly miss the curious architecture of a large house on the right which shouts 'Victoria!' Immediately after this bleak relic turn up a side lane on the right (map reference: 017/805) and in 70 yards (65 metres) gain the footpath which leads up through a farm which can be very muddy in wet weather. Over the brow at the far end is the Roosdyche.

A first sight of this long 'vale' sweeping off to the north gives me the impression that this is the work of Capability Brown. Roosdyche is a valley upon the western hill slope, ¾ mile (1 km) from north to south and about 120 feet (36 metres) wide. The banks on either side are up to 30 feet (8 metres) high and clothed with trees. The floor is surprisingly level and covered with grass. A long time ago the place was seriously thought to be the remains of a Roman Rhedagna or chariot course, with the ruined goal as a grassy hummock in the centre and the stables in tributary dikes. Today it is thought to be nothing more than a freakish natural formation.

Roosdyche would almost certainly seem to be a landslip on an extensive front, similar to (though bigger than) one found in Burrs Wood on the eastern edge of the National Park, and not so dramatic as the likewise-formed Alport Castles (see 'In Alport Dale').

At the extreme northern end climb the eastern bank up to a stile on the wall. Here you have an extensive view north over Buxworth to Chinley Churn and south-west across the Goyt Valley to Todd Brook Reservoir. Climb the stile and keep along the bottom of this first, then down the left-hand edge of the next and so over another stile by a gate onto the lane between Whaley Bridge and Buxworth at 669 feet (209 metres) above sea level (map reference: 017/817).

Turn right along Silk Hill Lane past cosy Silk Hill Farm and so down the 1-in-6 Silk Hill, cobbled and sunken and rather spoilt now by the thundering traffic on the Chapel-en-le-Frith bypass (A6). After crossing over the Buxworth Basin (a now restored arm of the Peak Forest Canal) you pass the old Navigation Inn and then reach the main road. This is **Buxworth** (not so many years ago called Bugsworth but the self-conscious community had the name changed), and as you climb towards the railway bridge ahead look at the remains of a disused tunnel on the left, just above the disused chapel. This gave access to a quarry from which stone was taken to the canal wharf for building purposes. Go under the railway bridge by Buxworth station and take the first lane on the left (map reference: 025/824).

After a ½ mile (0.75 km) uphill walk turn right at the first cottages, up the dip slope of Chinley Churn's escarpment. There is a 700 foot (213 metre) ascent ahead. Soon a pink-washed farmhouse (date 1654) is passed, above which the lane steepens appreciably. Not far below the next lane junction you can pick out a Roosdyche-in-miniature, just over the left-hand wall and under a single hawthorn. It is a tiny, grass-covered landslip but illustrates plainly how the Roosdyche was probably formed.

At the bleak junction above (map reference: 027/834) turn sharply right. You are now walking along the boundary of the National Park and will soon be within it.

Steeply down the lane and where the bold, craggy profile of **Chinley Churn** first appears look for the stile in the left-hand wall (map reference: 034/831). Climb the stile and walk up through the gorse banks beneath the gritstone edge. Here there is much evidence of man's labours. Many of the factories and railway constructions erected in the nineteenth century in the valley below were built from stone hewn here at Cracken Edge Quarry. Rabbits are the only tenants now!

Only after climbing the edge do you realise that the trig point topped Churn – said to be a corruption of 'cairn' – is still higher a distance to the west. From the 1480 foot (451 metres) summit of the Churn walk to the north-east and down to the footpath which runs north under the escarpment, dramatised by the long-dead quarrymen.

Beyond Whiterakes the lane becomes a track and you follow this to Hills House (map reference: 048/850). This is a sedate sort of place, sitting upon the watershed between Chinley and Hayfield. The garden has an ash tree surround, while a carved plaque over the front door contains a glass panel which presumably represents an eye. Known locally as 'Peep-o-day' this 'eye' is said to be set so as to allow the entry of the rays of the rising sun on certain days of the year.

A few yards further on the road between Chapel-en-le-Frith and Hayfield (A624) is gained. Turn left, then right in 100 yards (30 metres) up a lane towards Mount Famine. Soon a cross-roads is reached. You go straight ahead, towards the Sett Valley. If you prefer a high level route into the Edale Valley turn right at the cross-roads, up onto Mount Famine (map reference: 056/849) under South Head's summit and up the long western ridge of **Brown Knoll** (1866 feet/569 metres) to the top and so by Horsehill Tor and Colbourne to the ancient track between Chapel-en-le-Frith and Edale called Chapel Gate (map reference: 099/833). Turning east it is not a long walk down into the Edale Valley.

If you go straight ahead at the cross-roads below Mount Famine a slight rise brings you round a shoulder from where there is a clear downward view to the River Sett at Coldwell Clough, and the track soon to be taken in the clough-bottom.

Down the lane, go sharply right and so up the lane, noticing the almost unbelievable height of Mount Famine from the riverside. Above the steepest incline you reach an old farm on the left (map reference: 057/859). Newly erected in front of the farmhouse is an old sundial of Edward Bredbury on a carved gritstone post with the date '1706' and the initials 'EB'. Carvings abound here – a gritstone dog astride a barn roof ridge, a carved ball on the farmyard wall, initials on the door lintel and on either side of a large flowering plant carved over an outhouse door.

A little distance beyond this steading the hard road ends on a low bridge with a pointed tunnel-arch typical of many bridges in this depression. Continue straight ahead up the old trackway and in 1½ miles (2.5 km) of uphill walking you reach the pass between Hayfield and Edale, at **Edale Cross** a little over 1750 feet (541 metres) above sea level.

On the left-hand side of the track, by a gate, the old cross still stands. Most likely it served as a marker on the packhorse road called the Monk's road and would have been erected in medieval times by Cistercian monks. On a wild day, especially in winter, it is easy to imagine this situation as the dwelling of Boreas, personification of the north wind.

Carry on, over and down to the steep slope above the River Noe called **Jacob's Ladder** (named after the route's pioneer Jacob Marshall, and not linked officially with any Biblical steep!). This is one of the most popular approaches to the high plateau and is best avoided on a fine Sunday, especially in summer.

Once across the packhorse bridge below the Ladder you can look across and up to the west and see the almost-level ruins of Edale Head House. Fifty years ago this farm was standing intact, though empty. To me it always characterised the remote and romantic and has been a favourite dwelling site since my childhood. Go on again, reaching Upper Booth in less than 1½ miles (2.5 km), just after crossing Crowden Brook (map reference: 103/854). The last house on the Edale side of this hamlet is Crowden Lea. This is a Tudor house which dates to 1587, at least, and was the home of the Edale Shirts for many generations.

Then along the lane through **Barber Booth** to Edale proper, the centre of which is really Grinds Brook Booth. Booth is the old local name for a hamlet of farms and cottages, hence Upper, Barber, Grinds Brook and Nether (or Lower) Booths in this valley.

From Chinley and Whaley Bridge, continue over Chinley Churn and Edale Cross to **Edale**; the walk has been entirely over carboniferous grits and shales. In grey weather some would call it a drab-coloured route, but no drabber than any other Peakland route in such conditions. There are always colours in detail, lichen-covered farm buildings, dead bracken and water. On a bright day the views will long be remembered, especially towards the west.

WALK 13

Lyme Park, Sponds Hill and Kettleshulme

Outline:	**Lyme Hall, Bowstonegate, Sponds Hill, Charles Head, Kettleshulme, Whaley Moor, Lyme Hall**
Map:	**OS 1:25,000 Outdoor Leisure Sheet 1 'The Peak District – Dark Peak area'**
	OS 1:25,000 Outdoor Leisure Sheet 24 'The Peak District – White Peak area'
Distance:	**9½ miles/15.25 km**
Parking:	**Lyme Park car park**

This is the first of four walks in the western arm of the National Park area, that upland finger pointing out to the Cheshire Plain from the palm of the Pennines. For me, these are perhaps my favourite hill haunts – high, russet hills and green hollows, old houses and far prospects to the west.

Route

The main gates of Lyme Hall are ½ mile (0.75 km) west of Disley railway station. The drive is almost 1¾ miles (3 km) long, up to the car park below the Hall (map reference: 965/824).

The Legh family lived here from 1346 to 1946, when Robert Legh

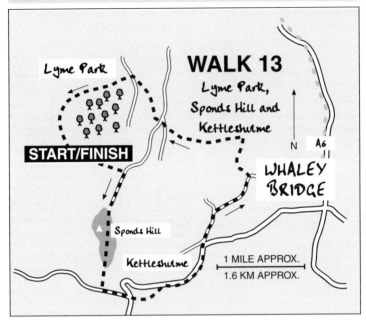

WALK 13

Lyme Park

Lyme Park,
Sponds Hill and
Kettleshulme

N   A6

WHALEY
BRIDGE

START/FINISH

Sponds Hill

Kettleshulme

1 MILE APPROX.
1.6 KM APPROX.

(third Lord Newton) gave the Hall and park to the National Trust. Today everyone can enjoy the graceful proportions and contents of the great house and its park, set on the western edge of the Peak Park.

From the car park below the Hall – there are two Big Trees (*Sequoia gigantea*) standing close together to the west – turn off left in 70 yards (64 metres), up to a gate and stile. Walk up the park drive beyond the gate for ¼ mile (0.5 km) keeping to the right (outside) of the park wall. Behind, above the park trees, you will see the conspicuous Lyme Cage atop Cage Hill, built about 1525. This was most likely erected for the ladies of the Hall to watch the progress of the hunt 'without the risks of horseback and with only the fatigue which follows the ascent of the many steps to the balcony'. It might, though, well have been used for the detention of poachers in this game-rich district.

Soon you go through a gate into the woodland and pass along the drive. At the far end of this sylvan drive you climb the stile near a gate through the high wall that marks the boundary of **Lyme Park**. This leads out onto the open moors now, with views ahead to Sponds Hill and Dale Top.

Go up the rutted track ahead to Bowstonegate Farm, standing on the watershed, whitewashed and well seen from miles around (map reference: 974/814). Close by the track here are the Bow Stones, two smooth pillars 3 feet (1 metre) high. Their lean suggests great age and may have led to their present name, signifying a bend or lean; were they markers on the ancient track from Disley towards Bollington? One authority believes them to have been used for bending longbows for the purpose of stringing them here in this former Royal Forest.

From the Bow Stones on a clear day extensive views can be enjoyed south to Shining Tor and Shutlingsloe (the latter 7½ miles/12 km away); to the east the next hill is Black Hill (1338 feet/407 metres) where you walk later. Behind that is the dark mass of Kinder Scout 8 miles (12.5 km) distant on the north-eastern horizon.

Lyme Hall from the west

Turn right along the rough lane, through a gate, then straight on along the track-way to a gateway near the summit of **Sponds Hill**. The trig point is only a stone's throw away to the west and the view from it extends on a clear day to the Welsh border, the Dee and Mersey estuaries and up the wooded, chimney-dotted valleys on the western slopes of Kinder Scout and Combs Moss. Here you are exactly 10 feet (3 metres) higher than the top of Black Hill, some way to the north-east.

Go on through the gate, on, over and down to the lane from the B5470 to Pott Shrigley. Turn left along the lane with views ahead to Windgather and soon the B5470 (Whaley Bridge–Macclesfield) road is joined at Charles Head. Across the main road are two stiles; take the left-hand one which contours round the hill-slope for about ¼ mile (0.5 km) then continue down the smooth ridge, dropping by scattered hawthorns to a stile in the bottom corner of the rough pasture, and passing over this and the little bridge over Todd Brook, overhung by alders. Just on the left here, a few yards downstream, is the larger arch of Reed Bridge carrying the main road over the brook.

Turn right up the road for ½ mile (0.75 km) to **Kettleshulme** village. A hundred yards (90 metres) beyond the fifteenth-century Swan Inn fork left, down a hard-surfaced lane, joining Kishfield Lane soon and so on for ½ mile (0.75 km). Fork right, dropping steadily down and over Todd Brook again by a typical stone single-arch bridge. You are now out of the Peak District National Park.

Climb the steep lane ahead past a gravel quarry on the right where the lane levels out. Fork left here up the gravel lane ahead. Straight ahead is the brow of Black Hill. A path soon slants off to the right, up the slope towards Whaley Moor. On this grass ridge stands the Plague or Dipping Stone, a squat stone with two hollows carved in its top. Presumably clear spring water was placed here to cleanse the plague-ridden in days long ago, or to disinfect plague victims' money so that 'clean' people could buy food and place it nearby. Maybe the Plague Stone was the base of marker posts delineating secular boundaries because the Derbyshire–Cheshire boundary runs very close to its site.

The path continues to the north but some distance before reaching Whaley Lane take the path that comes snaking in from the west. Follow this round to Dissop Head. Cross the lane and follow the path that heads north-west to East Lodge, right at the edge of Lyme Park.

The plague stone on Whaley Moor

If you are walking this way at the end of a fine day the sunset's bright banners will be in front of you all the way back to the Hall; and the deer often graze here towards evening. In ½ mile (0.75 km) beyond the gates the drive brings you in sight of the old stables and, just beyond, Lyme Hall. To the north Lyme Cage still stands obelisk-like against the sky on top of smooth, swelling Cage Hill.

WALK 14

Goyt Valley, Jenkin Chapel and Kettleshulme

Outline:	**Whaley Bridge, Taxal, Goyt Dale, Errwood Hall, Thursbitch, Eaves Farm, Nab End, Jenkin Chapel, Kettleshulme, Hawkhurst Head, Whaley Bridge**
Map:	**OS 1:25,000 Outdoor Leisure Sheet 1 'The Peak District – Dark Peak area'**

	OS 1:25,000 Outdoor Leisure Sheet 24 'The Peak District – White Peak area'
Distance:	13 miles/20.5 km
Parking:	Whaley Bridge railway station or Horwich End

This walk follows one dale towards its head, crosses a high moorland watershed and so down another dale to the starting point, a round of wooded valley and wild hill scenery and history of one kind and another.

Route

From the cross-roads at **Horwich End** (Whaley Bridge) (map reference: 011/807) walk up the steep road towards Macclesfield (B5470) for 600 yards (550 metres) and turn left along the lane to Taxal. This little hamlet is of great antiquity and as you pass the church of St James notice the gargoyles and tiny windows in the tower, and the newer nave and chancel.

Turn left immediately beyond the church, down into the **Goyt Valley**, passing between two still, tree-shaded fish ponds with Taxal Lodge perched overlooking the dale. Cross the footbridge, turn right and zigzag up through the trees, bearing right in a few yards through a gate. You now walk on up the dale-bottom past some fine beeches and conifers and the little footbridge leading to the lonely cleft of Normanwood. Soon notice a sharp bend in the river with a deep pool and above this erosion of the steep bank has exposed a big section of up-folded strata.

Keep along the hard track and the grass slope of **Fernilee Reservoir** rears straight ahead. Pass the filter house and go up the boulevard-like drive, swinging up through the trees to the top of the impounding wall where you turn south (right) along the eastern shore of the reservoir.

Stockport Corporation Water Board purchased most of the land on either side of the dale, and since the reservoir's completion in 1937 none of the farms and cottages have been inhabited; little remains save tumbled stones and the unaffected sheltering trees near each old house. There was Upper Hall, Brownhill Farm, Nook Farm, Errwood and Intake among others. When the reservoir almost dried up in the memorable summer of 1959 the old fields grew grass again and sheep were grazing there. An old plough stood by a gateway, where it had been left nearly a quarter of a century earlier.

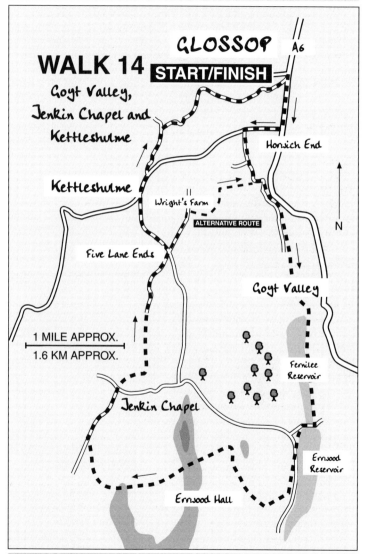

GLOSSOP
A6

WALK 14 START/FINISH

Goyt Valley,
Jenkin Chapel and
Kettleshulme

Horwich End

Kettleshulme

Wright's Farm

ALTERNATIVE ROUTE

N

Five Lane Ends

Goyt Valley

1 MILE APPROX.
1.6 KM APPROX.

Fernilee Reservoir

Jenkin Chapel

Errwood Reservoir

Errwood Hall

As you walk along this eastern shore you are actually following the old track of the Cromford and High Peak Railway which was completed in 1826. The Peak Forest Canal terminated at Whaley Bridge and the Cromford Canal ascended the Derwent Valley no farther than Cromford, and this railway was built over central Peakland to link the two canals. That this steeply-inclined trade route was considered more of a canal than a normal railway is seen by the fact that most of the intermediate station names were followed by the word 'Wharf'.

Ahead rears the impounding wall of the newer **Errwood Reservoir**. Soon notice the former 400 foot (122 metre) incline up onto Wild Moor to the south-east up which the railway climbed *en route* to Cromford. It is now used by the public road that crosses the valley using the top of the Errwood Reservoir impounding wall.

Cross the top of the impounding wall to the west side and head south on the lane skirting the reservoir's west shore before turning up the former drive to **Errwood Hall**, once a noble Peak District 'seat'. Walk up the drive through a wonderful world of rhododendrons and conifers – some of the finest Scots pines in the area – until you turn right, round a large Chile pine (Monkey Puzzle) and onto the level terrace in front of the ruined hall.

It is not certain when Errwood Hall was built by Samuel Grimshaw, but it would seem to have been before 1875, though not long before. Built and turreted in the Italian style, the house was dominated by a central tower above the main entrance. The level lawn lies to the south of the house and above it terraced walks lead to the sheltering hilltop where the Grimshaw family graveyard is sited.

Though very rich, Samuel Grimshaw was a devout Roman Catholic, and when the London North Western Railway Company wished to bring their line from Manchester to Buxton via the Goyt Valley they found such plans impossible to implement as this conservative landowner refused to allow such a 'godless invention' to pass over his land. Consequently the line was re-routed via Combs and Dove Holes, a more expensive and circuitous undertaking.

From near Errwood Hall there is a splendid view east down the tributary clough up which you have just come. It is not hard to believe that 40,000 rhododendrons were originally planted in the grounds.

The last member of the Grimshaw family left Errwood in 1930 and

Stockport Corporation bought the estate together with all those farms which likewise now stand derelict. Seven years later the Fernilee Reservoir was completed and the Goyt began to flood its dale. The Errwood Reservoir followed in the sixties.

To view the Grimshaw graveyard take the steps leading up from the south lawn in front of the house and through the rhododendrons and on the small hilltop behind you will find the iron railings forming an enclosure for the graves. Looking down towards the south-west, into Shooter's Clough, you may pick out the old coal mine which provided fuel for the estate. This drift went into the hillside for 1 mile (1.5 km) exploiting a pocket of coal-bearing measures in the surrounding millstone grit.

From the graveyard go north-west down into the small clough which can be gained otherwise by going along past the house and by a winding shrubbery walk and down across the stream, where the coal-bearing shales are exposed again in a steep cliff on the left.

Walk up the clough, keeping to the right (true left) bank for 20 minutes – there is a good path over the moor-side and through the numerous copses of dying trees. A ruined farmhouse is eventually reached and just beyond, sheltered by Scots pines, is the delightful shrine of the Grimshaws (map reference: 003/758). Besides a private chapel and resident priest this devout family had this charming circular chapel erected in 1889, dedicated to Saint Joseph. The romance continues – Delores, the beautiful Spanish companion to Mrs Grimshaw, probably painted the mosaic above the little alter for her initials appear beneath the inscription: 'Nunca se le Invoca envano a San Jose prueba de gratitud' ('No one asks in vain of Saint Joseph. A token of gratitude'). Lovely Delores was not strong and died at Lourdes, presumably seeking healing there.

Make towards the south-west from here, directly across the moor keeping in line with the door of the shrine, to the broken-down wall on the skyline. Crossing the wall you go into Cheshire and directly below is derelict Thursbitch Farm, long deserted at the head of this wild, backwater valley. Shutlingsloe is just visible to the south, 5 miles (8 km) distant.

Drop down the steep and even slope to Thursbitch, where you will see that little remains of standing walls – there was a very high barn wall on the west end of the buildings until the severe frosts of early 1963.

Jenkin Chapel

Cross the stream and go straight up the farther slope west, crossing the fence at a gate and so over the brow of the hill at 1530 feet (466 metres) above sea level. To the west Lamaload Reservoir blocks the River Dean's upper reaches and beyond a suggestion of the Cheshire Plain. Below is derelict Eaves Farm, and to the right Redmoor Farm, with tree-girt Jenkin Chapel beyond.

Go through the yard of Eaves Farm and along the green lane to Nab End (map reference: 979/758). At this hilly lane junction turn right towards Kettleshulme and in 10 minutes the lane bends down to Saltersford Hall (1593 over one door and the carved initials 'H.I.' over another door). Continue up the lane to pretty **Jenkin Chapel** at another junction.

This chapel of St John the Baptist appears more like a house with a defensive tower at one end than a rural church. Tradition states that it was erected to look like a farmhouse so as not to attract attention in the days of Jesuit persecution. If this is authentic the lovely tower with unusual outside steps up to the belfry was a much later addition, the date 1733 appearing above the main entrance. Although Jenkin Chapel stands at over 1050 feet (320 metres) it appears sheltered by the higher slopes to east and west and by the sycamores in the rectangular graveyard.

Across the lane is a stile into the fields. Cross these fields diagonally. making for Green Stack Farm – walk round the back of the farm and go across two grass fields to a barn. Down now to Dunge Farm, sheltered in a hollow by tall trees and well known these days for its beautiful gardens, and so along the lane to **Five Lane Ends** (map reference: 993/787).

At Five Lane Ends turn left down to **Kettleshulme**, 1 mile (1.5 km) away. Once in the village walk towards Whaley Bridge and turn left and so down Kishfield Lane, over Todd Brook and up to Hawkhurst Head. Keeping right the lane soon drops steeply above the Todd Brook Reservoir and so down into Whaley Bridge.

To shorten this route take the lane signposted 'Whaley Bridge' at Five Lane Ends. In less than ¾ mile (1.25 km) (opposite the gate to Wright's Farm) climb the stile on the right and cross the little pass in the ridge (and the Cheshire–Derbyshire border) to descend to the lane to Taxal. A short walk by this lane, or down the fields, brings you to Taxal, from where it is a short step down into Whaley Bridge.

WALK 15

Wildboarclough and the Dane Valley

Outline:	Wildboarclough, Tagsclough Hill, Gradbach, Lud's Church, Hangingstone, Danebridge, Wincle, Wildboarclough
Map:	OS Outdoor Leisure Sheet 24 'The Peak District – White Peak area'
Distance:	9 miles/14.5 km
Parking:	Wildboarclough bridge at riverside road junction (Map ref: 983/687)

Wildboarclough (map reference: 985/687) is something of a unique village, sheltered in the valley-bottom and protected to the west by that finest Peakland hill, Shutlingsloe, and the shoulders of Birchenough Hill and Wood Moss on the east. High deciduous trees

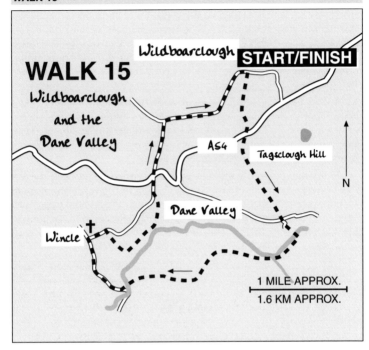

WALK 15

Wildboarclough
and the
Dane Valley

Wildboarclough

START/FINISH

A54

Tagsclough Hill

Dane Valley

Wincle

N

1 MILE APPROX.

1.6 KM APPROX.

wind along the base of the clough and hide the scattered houses, many built as the result of mill developments in the past. It was here in 1737 that the young James Brindley was put in charge of the making and installation of the machinery by his employer, Abraham Bennett of Sutton, near Macclesfield. Up behind the village stands Crag Hall and in its park is a lake which served as the mill supply dam as well as decoration for the squire. There were three mills, on different levels, each driven by wheels which were turned by water from the wheel above – sheer economy and, to quote the late Bessie Bunker, 'No dirt, no noise, no fumes'. The building of the Wildboarclough mills was the turning point in Brindley's career. Today only the foundations of the mill below the arch bridge remain, by the Clough Brook.

Route

Up the lane towards Crag Hall is the former post office, once the largest rural post office in the country, a Georgian remnant of mill days. A little way above this is the church of St Saviour, pink with local gritstone and well sheltered by mixed trees.

Only a few yards above the post office turn off the lane to the right by cottages and proceed along the grassy lane, through a stile, across a pasture and at the far side turn up left and diagonally up right across the following pasture to a stile in the far corner beneath a stand of mature deciduous trees. Look back to the north-west, to the wide views of Shutlingsloe and the head of Wildboarclough.

Go up the narrow lane ahead and out across fields, skirting the top side of a plantation of Norway spruce. Contouring brings you through the farmyard of **Tagsclough**, the farm with a ruined house but outbuildings in good repair and still in use. The lane, often waterlogged, soon brings you onto the Buxton–Congleton road (A54) 1 mile (1.5 km) above Allgreave.

The view of Shutlingsloe with Wildboarclough beneath is really wonderful from here on a clear day, sun or cloud, summer or snow. The hill is a true cone when viewed from any point of the compass – the geographer's idea of a model conical hill – but made unique by that characteristic 'crook' of slope near the summit on its eastern side, that lovely 30 foot (9 metre) upthrust of gritstone outcrop to the very top.

Cross the main road and up through rough pasture for a few yards to join the lane running over the shoulder of Birchenough Hill (a little over 1500 feet/457 metres) to Burntcliff Top on the Flash road. Very soon along the lane fork left onto a poorer, grassy lane where you will soon have wide views west, to the Cloud and Mow Cop (topped by its folly looking out over the Cheshire Plain).

A little before Burntcliff Top is reached look to the south (front right) and notice the depression running parallel with the top of the wood on the opposite hillside. You will be visiting this area soon, to seek the mystery hidden there.

There is an old farmhouse at Burntcliff Top, on the roadside (map reference: 991/664). Until 1919 this was an inn – the Eagle and Child – and the carved inn sign over the front door can still be seen, together with another carving of an eagle in the porch.

By the side of the outbuildings across the road is a gate. Go through this and down the lane past a farm. Turn left at a barn below the farm and climb the wall near a gate. In a few yards a short section of wall protecting four old stone troughs is seen on the left. These troughs are filled with running spring water and were placed here for the use of packhorses employed in the carrying of wool and woollen goods to and from the old Gradbach Mill on the valley floor below.

Go steeply down the packhorse track now and over the new foot-bridge over the young River Dane, crossing from Cheshire into Staffordshire. Here is Gradbach Mill, now a Youth Hostel. Walk round the front of the mill to look at the large water-wheel recess (the wheel has long since been removed).

Along the path by the left bank of the river, pass the house where the mill manager once lived. Behind the house is a stile leading into pasture fields. Walk along for a further ¼ mile (0.5 km) to a footpath over the Black Brook (map reference: 991/658). Straight ahead is a steep slope covered by mixed woodland – oak, larch and Scots pine predominate. Climb for 50 feet (15 metres) then turn up right along a good path through the trees for about ⅓ mile (0.5 km).

You are near the secret held by these hill-angles, and upon reaching a castle-like outcrop of gritstone to the right of the path – Castle Cliff Rocks – look for a path running back to the left. Follow this back and in 150 yards (135 metres) look out on the right for a narrow tunnel-like entrance through the rocks to Lud's Church.

A fault in the millstone grit has been widened by a landslip similar, though on a smaller scale, to that responsible for Alport Castles. Beyond the entrance you can turn left or right. On the left a flight of steps cut from the rock floor takes you down to the bed of the 'Church'. The walls on either side are 60 feet (18 metres) high, less than 3 yards (2.5 metres) apart and this section – 'The Nave' – is 600 feet (182 metres) long. Ferns and other shade-loving plants cloak the walls and the place is always dank. It is said that snow lies here throughout the summer in some years and there is a record of a local man opening a bag of snow in the centre of Leek on 7 July 300 years ago, snow collected no doubt from this 'crevisse in the steepe hilles'.

If you continue to the far end a short flight of steps will bring you out onto the heather moor behind, but by scrambling on to the very end

Inside Lud's Church

of the fault you will find a deep cave.

By turning to the right upon entering the 'Church' you will find a smaller 'nave' and another cave at the far end. One explorer is recorded to have found Druidical remains within, another states that water was heard in the distance, but I do not know that anyone has ever explored the cave properly.

There are plenty of legends about Lud's Church, some quite recent, others of great antiquity. Of the former kind is the tale about Squire Trafford of Swythamley which states that he was galloping his horse while hunting and realised that he was approaching the top of the chasm at too great a speed to stop so jumped his horse across – successfully, though some of his hounds were killed in their fall to the floor of 'The Nave'. You may still inspect Trafford's Leap.

The chasm got its name from Walter de Lud-auk, the leader of Wycliffe's supporters in these hills and valleys, the Lollards, in the fourteenth century. In a struggle with soldiers in the 'Church' Walter's beautiful granddaughter, Alice, was killed and buried beneath venerable roots, a forceful reminder of the Reformation. It is certainly likely that such a natural hide-out would be used by zealous Reformers in those days of cruel persecution.

The fourteenth-century poet who wrote 'Sir Gawain and the Green Knight' probably visited this place and created his poem with it in mind; certainly the descriptions contained therein describe the country from Swythamley Park to Lud's Church and recent research seems to come down conclusively in favour of this location.

Coming out of the main entrance you have fine views across the **Dane Valley** to Helmsley Farm, Windyharbour and the very tip of Shutlingsloe peeping beyond on a clear day. Walk back along the path to Castle Cliff Rocks and keep straight on to the west. In about ¾ mile (1.25 km) the track breasts a little col where a wide view opens revealing the pastoral Churnet Valley to the south, with Leek at its mouth 6 miles (9.5 km) away. Up on the left are the Roaches, and Gun Hill across the valley in front.

Very soon the lane curves round past a farm, and soon again go through a gate. Go straight on here (map reference: 975/653), leaving the main lane where it turns down left. Along the rougher lane ahead notice the bold Hanging Stone up on the right-hand skyline. This grit-stone outcrop contains two remembrance plaques, one to Lt-Col. Conley Brocklehurst of the Royal Hussars, erected in 1949. The other on the western face is a stone slab to 'Burke', mastiff of the Swythamley Squire.

The lane passes above ancient Hanging Stone Farm and soon bends sharply to the right. At the bend keep straight down through a gateway and halfway down the first field go left through a gap in the left wall where cows have worn a path. Make down at 45 degrees from this gap to another gap in the wall at the bottom and down the rough bank, making down to the main path contouring above the River Dane. Turn left along the path on reaching it, which eventually drops to river level (notice the tilted, shaly strata) and rises up a short lane to the Wincle–Heaton road at Danebridge (map reference: 965/652).

Turn right over the bridge and cross from Staffordshire to Cheshire. Up the hill to **Wincle**. At Wincle church turn right and in ⅛ mile (0.25 km), at the foot of a steep hill, right again down the first lane leading towards the valley. Go down and down until the lane turns sharply to the right, to a farm. Here climb the stile ahead and turn sharply to the left, along the slope.

As an alternative to the above look for a flight of stone steps in the high right-hand wall a few yards above the Ship Inn on the steep climb approaching Wincle from Danebridge. Climb these steps and follow the path through one field, keeping over to the left, and make for a fine group of larch. Walk down into the plantation ahead and up the other side and across two more fields to a farm. Go through the yard and along the lane for 50 yards (45 metres), then climb the stile where the lane turns up left. This is where the alternative route converges.

Ahead lie the green woods and pastures of the Dane Valley, where I often think Delius heard his first cuckoo in spring! Keep along the path high above the Dane for about 1 mile (1.5 km) to Allmeadows Farm, where there are many troughs in a row in the yard, fed by a spring.

Out along the lane keep right to the cross-roads. Cross the Buxton–Congleton road (A54) and go along the lane for 1½ miles (2.5 km) by the Clough Brook, back to **Wildboarclough** village where your route began.

WALK 16

Shutlingsloe and Macclesfield Forest

Outline:	Wildboarclough, Shutlingsloe, Langley, Walker Barn, Whitehill, Forest Chapel, Shutlingsloe, Wildboarclough
Maps:	OS Landranger 1:50,000 Sheet 118 'Stoke-on-Trent & Macclesfield' OS Outdoor Leisure 1:25,000 Sheet 24 'The Peak District – White Peak area'
Distance:	10 miles/16 km
Parking:	Wildboarclough bridge at riverside road junction (Map ref: 983/687)

Route

From the wooded depths of **Wildboarclough** (map reference: 985/687) climb the lane that leaves the main road opposite the downstream end of the demolished carpet mill. This leads across breezy, open pastures to

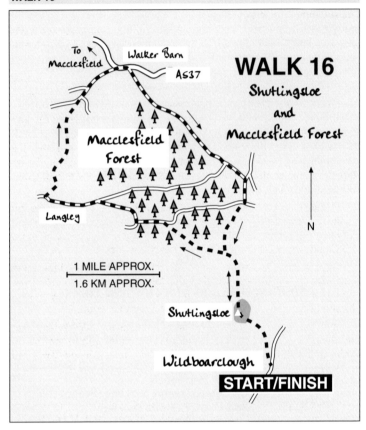

WALK 16
Shutlingsloe
and
Macclesfield Forest

To Macclesfield
Walker Barn
A537

Macclesfield Forest

Langley

1 MILE APPROX.
1.6 KM APPROX.

N

Shutlingsloe

Wildboarclough

START/FINISH

Shutlingsloe Farm (map reference: 982/695) below the crooked top of **Shutlingsloe**, finest of all Peak District hill shapes. No other in the National Park comes near to it for perfection of shape – Chrome Hill, north of Hollinsclough, perhaps comes closest. The footpath used to go through the yard at Shutlingsloe Farm but now turns up towards the summit somewhat earlier. The footpath signs make it clear and a steep pull up the east face soon brings you to the top.

The summit of Shutlingsloe

The gritstone cap of this hill is responsible for the characteristic 'crook' when viewed from the south-east, say on the A54 near Tagsclough Hill above Allgreave.

From this 1659 foot (505 metre) viewpoint there are remarkable vistas in clear weather, as good as any in the district. In the east (from north to south) is Shining Tor (1834 feet/559 metres) with the Buxton–Macclesfield highway below it; then comes the level brow of Cuckoo Rocks and Wood Moss with Axe Edge rising behind; the ragged crest of the Roaches lies in the south-east. Directly below you on this side is the green trench of Wildboarclough with Lord Derby's Crag Hall on the far slope. The ornamental lake in the grounds supplied the 'ladder' of James Brindley's mills below.

To the south is the thickly wooded trough of the Dane Valley and north Staffordshire beyond, swinging round to the uniquely named Wincle Minn and Bosley Minn. Thrusting out upon the Cheshire Plain is The Cloud with its antique earthwork below the top.

Over in the west are the green levels of the Cheshire Plain, often blue with haze. In clear weather the Jodrell Bank radio telescope catches the sun near Holmes Chapel. If very lucky you may have a glimpse of the River Mersey winding on towards Liverpool Bay.

In the north there is a pattern of fields at the head of Wildboarclough and the dark reaches of Macclesfield Forest, pulled up to the sky on White Hill, with Toot Hill licking the woods, a primeval tongue extended to the west.

Your route drops north from the summit and follows the 'improved' path over boggy ground all the way to the edge of **Macclesfield Forest**. The dense plantations hide the reservoirs below; they also conceal from view the remains of former isolated hill farms – Ferriser and Coombs – and the stone walls that once enclosed their steep pastures.

A broad path slants down north-west to reach the public road near the shore of Trentabank Reservoir, highest of the Langley trio. Go down the lane, skirting the middle dam where you are bound to see signs of waterfowl, before reaching **Langley**. This former mill village has rows of quaint cottages (in one of which was born the great wildlife artist Charles

F. Tunnicliffe, RA in 1901) but you turn right up the first narrow lane to the north bank of the third reservoir.

Now take the steep path that climbs all the way up to the summit of Tegg's Nose Quarry. Here among the heathery, former workings are gathered preserved machines from another age when gritstone was extracted to build and repair many of the farms, cottages and field boundaries in this east Cheshire hill country. There are more wonderful prospects to north and west in clear weather.

At the north-eastern end of Tegg's Nose you gain the original Buxton–Macclesfield high road and continue towards Buxton for ½ mile (0.8 km) to the hamlet of **Walker Barn**, beside the busy A537 at almost 1200 feet (365 metres) above sea level. The Setter Dog Inn was built here at the junction in 1740; earlier last century the Etchells farmed next door and sold a white cow to the Tunnicliffes. The son, Charles, painted this beautiful beast – it was always called 'Etchells'.

Go up the road towards Buxton for 100 yards (90 metres) then turn right up a steep, straight lane towards the Forest. In 1 mile (1.6 km) fork left at the northernmost point of the planted forest, along a track to gain the summit of White Hill (1550 feet/472 metres).

All the sweeping pastoral territory to the east, in the lee of the highest ground culminating in Shining Tor (1834 feet/559 metres), which is Cheshire's highest point, was taken in hand by Sir William Brereton in the late seventeenth century and turned into 2000 acres of sheepfolds, tenanted by local sheep farmers.

Continue down the track to Forest Chapel, a stone hamlet on an exposed col best known for St Stephen's church (rebuilt 1834). It is the second highest situated parish church in England, where the old rush-bearing ceremony takes place each August to remind us of the days when church floors were strewn with straw or rushes. More interesting is nearby Toot Hill, a mysterious earthwork that may well be the site of the original hunting lodge of Macclesfield Forest.

At Forest Chapel follow the lane south-east, down to the next junction. To the left is Bottom-of-the-Oven (coldest spot in the dale in winter), Macclesfield and Buxton but you turn right for ⅓ mile (0.5 km) to that draughty 1178 feet (359 metres) col where you will see the memorial tablet to the fondly remembered Macclesfield countryman and historian Walter Smith. In clear conditions there is a fine vista to the west, down through the plantations towards the Langley reservoirs.

A path ahead conducts you down into the depths of the forest, and the ruins of Ferriser Farm. It takes a strong imagination to visualise the look of this place when it was a beautifully sited working hill farm set in open pastures with broad vistas towards Macclesfield and the Cheshire Plain beyond. The path continues beyond Ferriser, roughly southwards through the trees to come out onto the open moor at the place where you went down towards the reservoirs earlier in the day.

Go back now along the restored path across the moor, aiming for the conspicuous cone of Shutlingsloe. At the foot of this summit pyramid you can look west again, over Oakenclough to High Moor and round the slope to empty Piggford Moor where traditionally witches swoop beneath the mellow light of the Hunter's Moon on calm October nights.

If you are lucky and reach Shutlingsloe's summit at sundown watch the descending light over five counties or more – always a reminder to me of childhood scrambles to this breathless knoll:

> *Break in the clouds*
> *And dapples beyond in the blue:*
> *Break in the clouds*
> *And a shaft of gold streams through,*
> *Escaping the lane of peace*
> *Where dreams are always new.*

CICERONE GUIDES TO THE AREA

WALKING IN THE SOUTH PENNINES   *Gladys Sellers*
  The area between the Dales and the Peak District. Rich in industrial heritage.
  ISBN 1 85284 041 2 400pp

WALKING IN THE WOLDS   *Charlie Emett*
  38 circular walks in tranquil East Yorkshire.
  ISBN 1 85284 136 2 296pp

THE YORKSHIRE DALES - A walker's guide to the National Park   *Gladys Sellers*
  A comprehensive survey of the best walking in the Yorkshire Dales.
  ISBN 1 85284 097 8   328pp

"Star" FAMILY WALKS IN THE PEAK DISTRICT AND SOUTH YORKSHIRE   *John Spencer & Ann Beedham*
  52 short walks adapted from the Sheffield Star Weekend Walk column. 2-3 hours. Ideal for families.
  Winner of the COLA/OWG Best Guidebook 1998.
  ISBN 1 85284 257 1 64pp Wire Bound

HIGH PEAK WALKS   *Mark Richards*
  ISBN 0 902363 43 3 208pp PVC cover

WHITE PEAK WALKS Vol 1: THE NORTHERN DALES   *Mark Richards*
  ISBN 0 902363 53 0 192pp PVC cover

WHITE PEAK WALKS Vol 2: THE SOUTHERN DALES   *Mark Richards*
  ISBN 0 902363 88 3 288pp PVC cover
  A best-selling trilogy which covers the most popular walks in the Peak District. Mark Richards' style
  owes much to Wainwright, but here he proves equal to the master.

WHITE PEAK WAY   *Robert Haslam*
  An 80-mile walk through the Derbyshire Dales with full details of youth hostels, pubs, etc.
  ISBN 1 85284 056 0 96pp

WEEKEND WALKS IN THE PEAK DISTRICT   *John & Anne Nuttall*
  12 magnificent circular weekend outings illustrated with John's fine drawings.
  ISBN 1 85284 137 0 296pp

WALKING IN SHERWOOD FOREST & THE DUKERIES   *Elaine Burkinshaw*
  Walking in the heart of England in a rural mix of woodland, farms and parks. For all the family and
  readily accessible to the industrial midlands.
  ISBN 1 85284 279 2 128pp

WALKING IN STAFFORDSHIRE   *Julie Meech*
  40 walks of short and medium length, many in the Staffordshire Moorlands, a remote but accessible
  section of the Peak District.
  ISBN 1 85284 317 9